Inspire or Perish
Second Edition

Inspire or Perish

Second Edition

How to Communicate Your Message to a 21st Century Audience

Gerardo Suárez del Real Luján

Patrick Williams

Copyright © 2021 Sliding.ca Inc. All rights reserved. No part of this publication may be reproduced, or stored in a retrieval system, or transmitted in any form or by any means, electronic, mechanical, photocopying, recording, or otherwise, without express written permission of the authors.

Limit of Liability/Disclaimer of Warranty: This publication is designed to provide accurate and authoritative information in regard to the subject matter covered. It is sold with the understanding that neither the authors nor the publisher are engaged in rendering legal, investment, accounting or other professional services. While the publisher and authors have used their best efforts in preparing this book, they make no representations or warranties with respect to the accuracy or completeness of the contents of this book and specifically disclaim any implied warranties of merchantability or fitness for a particular purpose. No warranty may be created or extended by sales representatives or written sales materials. The advice and strategies contained herein may not be suitable for your situation. Neither the publisher nor the authors shall be liable for any loss of profit or any other commercial damages, including but not limited to special, incidental, consequential, personal, or other damages.

For general information on our other products and services, please contact us at info@Sliding.ca

ISBN-13: 978-1-7771768-2-2

Cover design by: Sliding.ca

To Carolina and Elizabeth

TABLE OF CONTENTS

1. INTRODUCTION	1
1.1. Persuade	2
1.1.1. Post-truth	5
The Online World	9
2. PREPARATION	13
2.1 Motivation	15
2.1.1 The Here and Now	17
2.1.2 Goal	19
2.1.3 Objectives	20
2.2 Know your Audience	23
2.2.1 Empathy	27
The Online World	29
3. CONTENT	37
3.1 The Triangle	40
3.2 Create your Message…	42
3.3 Types and Sub-types of Presentations	43
3.4 Discover the Metaphor	45
3.5 The Journey (Story)	47
3.6 Paper first	49
3.6.1 Sticky Notes	51
3.7 Medium	53
3.7.1 Slides, Flip Chart, White Board, or Speech	55
3.7.2 Prioritizing	58
3.7.3 Create a Handout	60

3.8 Design Principles	64
3.8.1 Slide Deck Content	64
3.8.2 Your Main Message	65
3.8.3 Bite-Size Slides	66
3.8.4 One Motif	68
3.8.4.1 Fonts	70
3.8.4.2 Colour	70
3.8.4.3 Images	71
3.8.4.4 Animations	74
The Online World	75
4. DELIVERY	**81**
4.1 Environment	83
4.2 Visual vs. Auditory	86
4.2.1 Visual	86
4.2.2 Auditory	89
4.3 The Show	91
4.3.1. Your Intro	91
4.3.2 Stage Craft	96
4.3.3 Be Magical	103
4.3.4 Speaking with Emotion	104
4.3.5 The Close	105
4.4 The 3G Method	107
The Online World	112
5. CONCLUSION	**119**
5.1 The 5Cs	119
5.2 Our Call to Action	124

Inspire or Perish
Second Edition

1. INTRODUCTION

Patrick Buys a Sound System

Standing outside the stereo store I was excited and ready to buy. Finally, I was ready to take the plunge and get that perfect home entertainment centre I'd been dreaming about for months. I had completed my research (sound requirements, price range, room layout) and had all the data I needed to make a logical and informed decision.

Confidently, I entered the store, found a sales rep, and handed him my list of requirements, the words "Patrick's Stereo Specs" emblazoned across the top of the page. He was impressed. Checking out my datasheet, he looked up and said to me, "Wow, you've really done your homework. I know the exact system that will suit your needs." Excellent! Following him to the back of the store, my excitement built. He took me straight to a gorgeous home entertainment system and began comparing my list of requirements to the datasheet I had given him. It was perfect, everything matched: stats, price, and even look.

I was just about to tell him to ring it up, and that's when it happened. A few feet to my left, in my peripheral vision, something caught my eye. It was another home entertainment system. It was somewhat similar to the one I was about to purchase but there was something different about it, something I couldn't put my finger on, something that drew me to it, like a moth to a flame. "How about that one?" I asked the sales rep. "You don't want that one" he replied. "Why not?" I asked. "Because it doesn't have a lot of the items on your list of requirements." Our back and forth went on for a very long time with the sales rep getting more and more frustrated. He was doing his level best to look out for my interests and I wouldn't get out of my own way. He knew I was being illogical and I knew I was being illogical, but I just couldn't stop eyeing that other system; more than that, I couldn't stop wanting that other system.

Contrary to the advice of my sales rep, and in opposition to my own self-interest, I ended up buying the second system. My emotions overruled my reasoning.

We like to think we're logical beings who make all our decisions based on the facts presented to us but, at our most basic, our emotions almost always trump our sense of logic[i].

That same principle holds true for an audience when they are watching and listening to a speech or a presentation. If the content runs counter to their core belief system or causes them emotional discord they may very well turn off and stop listening to the information being presented to them.

With that thought in mind, let's talk about presentations.

1.1. Persuade

Persuasion is Dead![ii]

Traditionally, people present in order to inform, entertain, persuade, or inspire. At Sliding.ca, we believe, as the 21st Century unfolds, the ability to persuade is being dramatically diminished. This is resulting in an increase in the need for presenters to inspire their audience in order to get their message across.

As time passes, we are seeing an exponential increase in our ability to communicate with each other. There are many, many advantages to these changes. We can now connect with our friends and relatives twenty-four hours a day and across the many miles that may separate us. We can now instantly access information that may previously have taken days to track down. We now have the ability to interact with acquaintances and strangers alike, in real time, as though they were actually right there sitting next to us. We are truly living in a marvelous age. But, along with the changes that are taking place, there are adjustments that have to be made. The same inventions and innovations that make it possible for us to reach out to the whole world also make it possible for us to become more insular. Many of us spend more of our time accessing information about only those things that personally interest us, or only paying attention to information, news, or opinions that we agree with.

There is so much data and stimuli bombarding us that we have developed the ability to tacitly filter out anything that we consider irrelevant or runs counter to our core belief system. Some people actually suffer from anxiety when presented with information that disagrees with their beliefs.

In a study conducted at Northwestern University it was found that, when people's confidence in their beliefs is shaken, they actually become stronger advocates for their beliefs[iii]. Applied to the world of speaking and presenting this raises the unsettling situation in which, the more persuasive the information you present to your audience, the more resistant they may be to its acceptance. Well, that can't be good! What do we do with all the information we've researched, organized, loaded into our persuasion cannons, and readied to shoot at our target audience?

We find another way, that's what we do. Our ability to persuade may be diminished but we still have the ability to inform, entertain, and inspire our audience, so let's maximize one, two or all three of those remaining "purposes for presenting" and deliver our message in a way that our audience will listen to, embrace, and remember for hours, days, months, and even years.

Every speech or presentation, to be effective, should contain a measure of inspiration. Many speeches are designed to be purely inspirational. To make our presentations even more powerful, we could combine entertainment with inspiration, or information with inspiration, or a combination of all three. By doing this, we dramatically increase our chances of having our audience listen to, accept, embrace, and remember the message we hope to share with them.

This leaves speakers and presenters in a situation in which they can no longer change minds with data, they have to appeal to them emotionally and inspire them to adopt your point of view, or at least allow them to soften their point of view.

When we speak about the three remaining purposes for presenting, to inform, to entertain, and to inspire, we believe that an effort to inspire your audience should always be integral to each presentation you create and deliver. Then, when entertainment, or information, or both are combined with inspiration we begin to see the real magic take place.

We live in an age in which we seem to be increasingly influenced by our emotions. In order to get an audience to pay attention to our message, we have to inspire them. We have to appeal to their emotions in some way and open their hearts and their minds. Rather than wasting our energy trying to persuade people with facts that they may be resistant to, we have to find a way to inspire them to rise above their present position and discover new, exciting, and non-threatening information on the issue before them. Only the audience can decide to change their point of view and accept your message and that decision has to be based on information they believe they have discovered on their own. The era of, what we call, the data cannon is obsolete.

One of the most difficult tasks facing presenters is delivering information. The problem faced when presenting to inform is the inherent limit on the ability of an audience to absorb and process the information. We suggest limiting the number of points you want the audience to remember to three. When you include the main message of the presentation that brings the total number of points for the audience to remember to four, a manageable number providing the main message and three points in a clear, concise, and compelling fashion.

1.1.1. Post-truth

We Defer to Emotions Over Logic

People have always been emotional creatures, and that is a good thing. If it weren't for our emotions, we wouldn't be able to function or make decisions. In a study cited in a 1999 Journal of Neuroscience article, Antonio Damasio[iv] and his associates shared a ground breaking discovery. Dr. Damasio and his team studied people who had suffered damage to the portion of the brain responsible for emotions. Incredibly, they found that these people had not only lost the ability to feel emotions, they had also lost their ability to make decisions. The people in the study didn't lose their powers of logical thought, they fully understood the options available to them; they just couldn't decide between them.

Mid-20th Century film is rife with the caricature of the stoic parent or grandparent who could never get in touch with their emotions. That caricature seems to be becoming a thing of the past. Now, as we begin the third decade of the 21st Century we, appear to be more and more motivated by our emotions and less and less motivated by our logic.

This point was driven home when The Oxford Dictionaries chose, as their Word of the Year for 2016, the word "post-truth.[v]" Post-truth is an adjective defined as 'relating to or denoting circumstances in which objective facts are less influential in shaping public opinion than appeals to emotion and personal belief.' To see post-truth in action we only have to look at the conduct of our 21st Century political campaigns, both here and abroad.

Another factor influencing our increasing emotionalism is the increasing complexity of knowledge. Accompanying the amazing change we have experienced in communications is the incredible wealth of information available to us everywhere we go. This change brings with it three important factors:

1. There are now so many sources of information that it is becoming increasingly difficult to try and establish empirical facts on any subject, especially, when the hierarchy of facts has been laid to waste by search engines such as Google or Bing.

2. When I was a boy (many, many years ago), if I wanted information about a particular topic, I would begin with The Encyclopaedia Britannica (now www.britannica.com) and then, if my question wasn't answered, I would head to the library. Today, we live in the flip side of that world. We have so many sources we just don't know where to start and then, when we perform a search, the information isn't even ranked according to veracity or credibility. Arriving at the truth has become a complex proposition, frequently an anxiety inducing proposition, and on occasion, an impossible proposition. Is it any wonder people find themselves recoiling from the facts?

3. Once we find a source of information we trust, we become more likely to return to that source time and time again. With no discerning word to contradict our self-reinforcing knowledge base we develop an ever-increasing bond with the facts presented to us. After hearing the same facts over and over again, our bond slowly evolves from an intellectual attachment to an emotional attachment. This attachment can

heighten to the point where any contradiction of that knowledge can result in physical anxiety.

In some situations, empirical data is actually being set aside in favour of group opinion. For example, Luis von Ahn[vi], one of the inventors of CAPTCHA (one of those little boxes with squiggly letters that you have to replicate to gain access to some websites), found another use for this system he co-invented.

Dr. van Ahn and his team were working on a herculean project to scan and digitize as many of the world's books as possible. The problem was that many of the older books had smudges on their pages and words that were difficult to decipher. To deal with this problem, they came up with an innovative and brilliant solution. Using CAPTCHA, they would scan the word they were having trouble with into a CAPTCHA-box and ask people trying to gain access to a protected site to retype the word. Then they would poll the results and opt for the spelling of the word that the greatest number of people selected. The savings in time were immense, and the system performed magnificently. There was, however, a side effect to their method. As effective and positive the benefits may have been, they were setting aside empirical knowledge in favour of knowledge arrived at based on the opinion of the majority of the group. Truth was being decided according to majority rule.

We are living in a world in which 'truth' is becoming less and less empirical. This new reality must be acknowledged and accounted for as we endeavour to educate, entertain, and inspire our audience.

The Online World

As we were preparing to publish Inspire or Perish, the world changed in a way no one anticipated. The COVID-19 virus swept across the planet and, with it, came the exponentially increasing need for people to effectively communicate with each other online.

In response to this recent development, we are reissuing Inspire or Perish with new material added to address the adaptations needed to take meetings, training, and presentations from the face-to-face world to the virtual world.

The technological availability required to hold an online event makes it seem like conducting a virtual session is super easy. However, doing it well is super difficult. That's why it's important to develop the habits we share with you in these appended sections.

As you read these added materials, keep in mind that almost all of what we share with you applies to both face-to-face and online sessions. To be comprehensive, we will repeat suggestions that apply to both environments. The additional techniques and principles that we share with you will help to make your online meetings, training, and presentations more professional and effective.

To make it easier to navigate, we have added this new material to the end of every chapter and tagged it with the label "**The Online World**."

Case Study: Aspire to Inspire

When we first spoke to Wendy, she was working on a presentation for non-profit boards. Her presentation was designed to convey the importance of board members working together as a unit in order to support the organization's work and to protect their reputation. Wendy's initial approach was to inform board members about the potential damage that could be done by board members acting on their own, independently, and inadvertently saying or doing something that could create embarrassment or legal difficulties for the organization. To accomplish this, her plan was to deliver a presentation that would instruct board members on the potential pitfalls they faced and then provide them with guidance on how to avoid those pitfalls. In effect, she was going to persuade them about the importance of being vigilant each and every day and whenever they represented the organization in public. In keeping with our belief that persuasion is dead, we suggested to Wendy that she could get a better and more enduring result if she endeavoured to inspire the board members rather than trying to persuade them.

To accomplish this goal, we set to work coming up with a metaphor and a simple message that the board members could relate to. Eventually, we decided to use the image of an umbrella to represent the idea that, at all times, the organization needed to be protected, and everyone on the board held the key to providing that protection. Accompanying the image of the umbrella, we came up with a question for the board members, rather than a directive. The question: "Am I acting in the best interest of the organization?" By presenting Wendy's audience with a message that inspired them to act we believed the buy-in would be much greater than if we tried to persuade them to act. We were right. Months later, after Wendy's presentation, the organization's board still remembered the message. Some of them even posted the image of the umbrella on the wall in their boardroom as a reminder of the message, and some used the "Am I acting in the best interest of the organization?" phrase as a mantra they would say out loud at the start of their meetings.

Persuasion is dead, inspiration endures.

Points to Consider

- When preparing a presentation, always consider the core belief system of your audience.

- To create a successful presentation, try to combine inspiration with education and entertainment.

With this in mind, the next chapter deals with the preparation and the decisions that must be made before turning ideas into reality.

Inspire or Perish

2. PREPARATION

Gerardo Builds a Boeing

When I was young, growing up in Guadalajara, Mexico, one of my hobbies was building model airplanes. A hobby long in my past, I was surprised when, on a visit home, my mother brought out two airplane models I hadn't seen or thought of in many years. Looking at the two models I was flooded with pleasant memories of the time I happily spent working on each of them. The earlier of the two models was a bright yellow P-17 Stearman biplane, while the latter was a B-17 Flying Fortress in US Air Force livery. I still remember the problems I had affixing the wing struts on the Stearman biplane.

One of the models was one of the first I'd ever built while the second was one of the last models I built. Needless to say, the difference in the precision, look, and dynamism of the two models was enormous.

The difference in the quality of the two builds didn't really surprise me, it had to be expected that, with experience, my hand would become steadier and my precision would improve. What stood out for me was the difference in the look and the dynamism of the two models.

The earlier of the two models, precision aside, had a functional, utilitarian appearance to it. The latter model looked more vibrant, more realistic, and much more alive. Struggling to figure out why my later work was so completely different, and better, than my earlier work, I flashed back to a blistering hot day in August of 1983.

It was my 14th birthday and my parents bought me a very expensive and very complicated Boeing CH-47 Chinook. It was amazing: twin-engine, tandem-rotor, lots of details; it was going to look fantastic. Beyond excited, I tore away the birthday wrapping, opened the box, pulled out the two main portions of the fuselage and glued them together. It was at that point that I looked down into the box and noticed the seats that were supposed to be inside. As soon as I saw those seats, I realized I'd made a big mistake. As I sat there, looking embarrassed and forlorn, my mother stood up and, walking past me, simply said "por no prepararte, te preparaste para fallar." The English translation: "By failing to prepare, you prepare to fail."

That simple, yet powerful, lesson has traveled with me ever since. Whether building more model airplanes as a youth, setting up a shoot as a fashion photographer, or creating a presentation for a client, the first word that always comes to mind is "preparation."

In this chapter, we will be discussing that very topic. From structuring your story, to marshalling your resources, to building your slide deck, to creating follow-up material, preparation will be the word of the day.

A few years after my mother shared that sage advice with me, I found out it was a quote from Benjamin Franklin. When I asked her where she first heard it, she told me she read it in a fortune cookie. She's my mother, so it must be true.

2.1 Motivation

Step 1. Answer the Question "Why am I Presenting?"

Just as we hope to motivate our audience it is important to get a handle on our own motivation for creating and presenting this particular presentation at this particular time. If you don't know your 'why,' the who, what, when, and where, will be meaningless. Preparedness begins with understanding your 'why.' We are all familiar with the old saying: if you don't know where you're going, how will you know when you get there? Well, similarly, the question can be asked: if you don't know why you're going, how will you know if you got there?

At Sliding.ca we always start with an overview and then, step by step, close in on our subject, as if we are ascending from the general to the specific. It's like moving from the outer rings of a dartboard towards the bull's eye, collecting information along the way. By the time you get to the center of the board you have a clear picture of what you're doing and, central to the success of your presentation, why you're doing it.

Let's go through the process. Initially, when it comes to understanding our motivation, we must ask ourselves, in the most basic sense: why do we want to do this presentation? When we ask our clients this question it is not uncommon to get the response: "Because my boss says I have to do it." In the final analysis, this may not be the most compelling motivation the presenter will need in order to effectively connect with his/her audience. However, it is a great place to start and serves to provide a clear understanding of the genesis of the project. Most importantly, it helps in understanding how to proceed as we ascend from one step to the next towards defining what we need to feel and do in order to stand before our audience and share our message with them.

Let's look at a few of those "outer ring" motivators: Is my basic motivation because my boss told me to do it, or could it be to impress my superiors in the company? Am I motivated by a need to entertain people, or to inform them of something, or to inspire them to take a particular course of action? Or, maybe I'm motivated by the desire to make money. Every one of these reasons is valid as a starting point and there are many, many other reasons that could fulfill the role of basic motivator.

Remember, we have only just begun our investigation and this is only the first step of the process. The next step is to go deeper and move through four of the W5 questions (who, when, where, why). Except, this time, we will attach the question 'why' to each of the W's.

Now that you have established your basic motivation for presenting, it's time to ask:

— "Why am I presenting to this audience (who) specifically?

— "Why am I presenting to this audience at this particular time (when)?

— "Why am I presenting at this particular venue (where)?

Finally, the most difficult question of all:

— "Why should this audience listen to what I have to say?" Or: "What's in it for them (WIIFT)?"

The answers to these questions will provide us with a guide book on how to approach our topic and how to make it relevant for our audience. Using the information we have gathered we can begin the process of fashioning our main message. This clear, concise, and compelling main message is going to act as the foundation for all that follows. As we build our presentation, we will use it to remind us that we're presenting in order to share something of value with our audience (the WIIFT). We will also use it to keep us on track, make sure we've left out nothing of importance to the audience, and to ensure that everything else in the presentation supports and helps to promote that message.

We think of the main message as "the gift" we have come to share with our audience. We will speak more about this in a later chapter.

2.1.1 The Here and Now

Why this Information, to These People, Today?

Now that we have decided upon our overarching reason for presenting, it is time to take a narrower view and, yet again, ask ourselves: *why?* Why are we presenting this specific presentation, to this specific audience, at this specific time, and in this specific venue? And, the most important question of all: how will this specific presentation help to support and move me closer to satisfying my overarching motivation?

If we don't ask and answer these questions it can be quite easy to get blown off course and end up where we had no intention of going. By staying focused on your overarching motivation, and then the *why* for each and every presentation you deliver, you will ensure that your efforts aren't being wasted and that everything you do moves you forward.

Audiences differ and circumstances change. If we aren't prepared to reassess our presentation and adapt or tweak it to ensure that it is appropriate for each particular occasion, we run the risk of going astray and wasting time and effort.

Imagine doing a presentation on "The Advantages of Flood Insurance" to two different audiences. One audience consists of people who live and work in a desert community. The second audience consists of people who live and work in a river valley. Now, imagine delivering the exact same presentation to both audiences. The life experiences of these two groups are going to be vastly different from each other, and they will, most likely, process the information much differently from each other.

Now, let's imagine delivering that same presentation to two audiences who both live in river valleys, except, one group has just lived through a devastating flood. Both audiences' existence might not be all that different but their current situation and mindset is definitely going to differ. As you walk into those two contrasting situations you better have done your research and be ready to bring empathy and compassion to whichever group you are speaking to.

Your *why* will change from presentation to presentation depending upon the circumstances and you have to be prepared to adjust and arrive at a clear understanding of why you're there and what you hope to accomplish. As Yogi Berra used to say: "If you don't know where you're going, you'll end up someplace else."

2.1.2 Goal

Step 2. Define a Broad Primary Outcome

Goals

Continuing with the example of the three groups of people: the desert dwellers, the river valley people, and the river valley people who had recently experienced a disaster. If your main message is about "The Advantages of Flood Insurance" it is time to consider everything you have learned about your audiences and decide upon an appropriate and realistic goal for each group.

Of the groups we mentioned, you would have to be a wild-eyed optimist to think that you could realistically sell the desert dwellers on "The Advantages of Flood Insurance."

It would be a different situation for the river valley group. That group might be eager to hear what you have to say and might actually come to your presentation predisposed to find out more about flood insurance and even sign up for a policy.

The third group, the river valley residents who have already been flooded out, may want to hear what you have to say but, in their case, you would probably be a little less than eager to consider selling them a policy.

Three different groups, three sets of circumstances, three mindsets, and three goals. As you prepare your presentations, be sure to set objectives that are targeted to the wants and needs of each individual audience. The key is to set goals that are realistic so that you can measure them, assess their viability, and adjust them to suit future presentations.

2.1.3 Objectives

Step 3. Establish Measurable Results (SMART)[vii]

Objectives are more specific to the event itself and serve to keep us on track. They also provide more immediate feedback regarding our progress and allow us to measure success at a later date.

A big (and frequently ignored) factor for the success or failure of almost any project, is the way its goals and objectives are stated and defined. In making all your goals and objectives meaningful and effective, the very popular SMART acronym is very handy. Every SMART objective should be:

Specific,

Measurable,

Achievable,

Relevant,

Time bound.

Before we continue, let's clarify that goals are more general than objectives because goals are set at a higher level than objectives. We could say that goals are strategic while objectives are tactical.

However, the SMART mnemonic applies to both goals and objectives.

When setting either a goal or an objective, always be as specific as possible. The biggest and most common mistake people make is to be vague or not as specific as they could be. Often, being specific is closely related to being measurable, however, they are not the same thing. For example, the objective "With this presentation I hope to achieve a great number of web hits on the landing page created for the event" is not specific enough because it only answers one of the 5W questions. It doesn't tell you the who, when, where, and why that will produce the desired result. Solve this problem by answering as many of the 5W questions as possible. In this particular case, the objective could be stated as "With the presentation to the 500 attendees of DevCON 2017 at the Sausalito Convention Centre, I hope to achieve a great number of web hits on the landing page created for the event and increase its public awareness." This objective is now specific but not yet measurable.

Being measurable is the most obvious of the five characteristics. As we discussed, the previous example is specific but not measurable because the phrase "a great number" is far too vague. In this case, you need to state exactly how many hits you are expecting to achieve; for instance, "With the presentation to the 500 attendees of FileMaker DevCON 2017 at the Sausalito Convention Centre, I hope to achieve three hundred unique web hits on the landing page created for the event and increase its public awareness." Now, you're actually measuring how many or how much you wish to achieve.

Whether getting 300 unique hits is possible or not falls into the realm of the achievable characteristic of the SMART mnemonic. Achievability will be determined based upon your, or somebody else's, experience or through market research. In the example given, if you determine that 300 unique hits are possible you can move forward; otherwise, adjust your forecast. A word of advice: do not set goals that are either too easy or too difficult to accomplish.

Another factor that could disincentivize you or your team, is the relevance of the goal or objective with regard to you and your team. If what you are trying to achieve doesn't matter to you and your team why would you put your heart and soul into it? Also, consider whether this is the right time to execute your plan, or even whether you are the right person to execute it.

The last part of the SMART "rule," is that the objective should be time-bound and refer to the target date of your goal or objective. In the example we have been discussing, the time-bound element depends on when you expect to get those 300 unique hits. This clearly affects the measurability and achievability of your goals and objectives. For instance, if you expect a seemingly reasonable objective to be achieved within an unrealistic timeframe, your target may no longer be "achievable."

Perhaps the not so SMART goal that we started with:

> "With this presentation I hope to achieve a great number of web hits on the landing page created for the event."

Would become SMARTer if it were stated like:

> "Within 30 days after the presentation to the 500 attendees of DevCON 2017 at the Susalito Convention Centre, I hope to achieve three hundred unique web hits on the landing page created for the event and increase its public awareness."

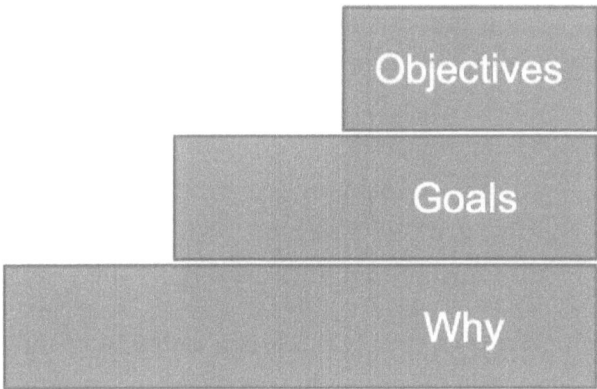

2.2 Know your Audience

WIIFT, culture, language, tone, emotional state

The importance of knowing your audience cannot be overstressed. You want to know everything you can about your audience before you begin to create your presentation. You must then keep all that information in mind as you create a presentation that speaks to them, specifically. And then, you must keep it all in mind as you prepare to deliver your presentation, and, yet again, as you actually deliver your presentation.

Here are some of the questions, in no order of importance, that you should be asking yourself as you prepare to create a presentation for a specific audience:

1. **What language do they speak?** When we say language we don't just mean in the English, French, Spanish, Mandarin, sense of language, but rather: what language do they speak in their profession? Do they use jargon particular to their occupation or line of interest? If you are speaking to a group of

sailors there's no advantage to using jargon or terminology commonly used by airline pilots. Do some research and, without straining the lines of credulity or making yourself out to be something you're not, use some terminology recognized by the sailors you are speaking to. It will help you to create a bond with your audience and make it easier for them to understand the concepts and ideas you're there to share with them.

2. **What is the underlying culture of your audience?** Just as with language, it is to your advantage to include references familiar to your audience that will make it easier for them to understand and embrace the message you hope to share. On the other hand, you want to, at all costs, avoid saying or doing something that your audience may find culturally offensive. Once you have offended an audience, especially culturally, you will find it almost impossible to regain their attention and their trust.

3. **What is the sensibility of your audience?** Sensibility may seem to be as obvious as language or culture, but it is still something that can be divined or sussed. For example, you wouldn't expect the same sensibility to be shared by an audience of animal rights activists as you would an audience of cattle ranchers. By knowing and understanding how the group you are speaking to views the world, you will be in a much better position to have them listen to and embrace you and your message.

4. **What is the emotional state of your audience?** We spoke earlier about the difference between how you would speak to a group of people who lived in the desert compared to a group of people who lived in a river valley who have just

experienced a flood. Imagine how differently your presentation would be received if you delivered it to the people living in a river valley before their homes were flooded. Knowing and constantly gauging the emotional state of your audience will help you to stay on their wavelength and increase your chances of honestly connecting with them.

5. **What creates resistance in my audience?** Every audience will have hot button topic that will cause them to erect a wall between them and the presenter. For example: sharing your perfect Martini recipe with a temperance group, or announcing executive bonuses at the same employee meeting that you're announcing layoffs. Understanding your audience's hot buttons will help you to adapt your message to your audience. Never ignore the elephant in the room.

6. **What motivates my audience?** What do they hope for in life; do they want to be rich, or fitter, or more successful? Maybe they hope for world peace, or a cleaner environment, or a better education for their kids. By knowing, as well as can be expected, what motivates them you'll have a better idea of how to speak to them and which parts of your presentation you should stress more than others.

7. **What inspires my audience?** We are all inspired by something. Once you have as clear an idea as possible regarding the language, culture, sensibility, emotional state, and motivations shared by your audience, it is time to ask yourself what, as a group, might inspire them. It could be a positive personality trait they see in others, such as: strength, perseverance, kindness, creativity, loyalty, independence, or optimism. Just like in the previous question, by knowing, as well as can be expected, what inspires your audience you'll have a better idea

of how to speak to them and which personality traits you should appeal to more than others. It should be noted that inspiration differs from motivation. Motivation deals more with the concrete aspects of life while inspiration is more of an emotional appeal.

How can I help my audience? From the moment you stand before an audience to the moment you leave the stage your primary concern should be to provide benefit to your audience. Even if you deliver a presentation confounded by unforeseen circumstances the fact that you were there for them, and not just for yourself, will earn goodwill and the satisfaction of knowing you tried your best to help them. By making the needs of the audience your primary goal you will ensure that each and every one of your presentations will be a success.

> **Note:** When it comes to the digestion of new information, people tend to be visually dominant. Your audience will be getting a lot more information from what they see before them than what they hear. Dress appropriately for the audience you're presenting to and the venue it will take place in. If you are giving a talk about roping cattle at the Calgary Stampede it makes no sense to turn up wearing a chef's hat and carrying a spatula.

Always keep in mind that every audience is unique.

That brings us to the power of empathy.

2.2.1 Empathy

Emotional Connection and Empathy Go Hand in Hand[viii]

In addition to having a very clear and concise understanding of what you want to say, the other key element is understanding how your audience perceives your message.

One of the biggest obstacles that presenters encounter when attempting to connect, inspire, and move an audience to action, is that they fail to picture themselves in circumstances their clients are experiencing at the particular time of the presentation. By doing this, they are failing to have empathy for their audience.

There are different ways to enhance empathic "skills." The very first step is to get to know the audience. What's in their past? How did they arrive at this point in time? What worries them? What calms them? What are the possible implications of your presentation? Will they resist your ideas? Have they recently gone through bad or less than perfect experiences? The more completely you understand your audience, the better.

Then, imagine how you would respond to your own idea or proposal under the same circumstances faced by your audience. Go deep and make a concerted effort to understand life as your listeners may be experiencing it. This will put you in a state of mind that will allow you to foresee potential rejection and, most importantly, it will highlight what you have in common with them.

By finding commonality and addressing the concerns of your audience you will be able to, first, create a main message that will resonate with them and deliver a presentation or speech that will inspire and move them to action.

Your empathy exercise should be as detailed and broad as possible. Ideally, it will inform every aspect of your presentation; aspects such as your choice of words, your language, what you will wear the day of the presentation, the colours, fonts and other graphic elements on your slides, the type of images, and so on.

An empathetic state of mind will also be very helpful when you deliver your presentation. It will help you to "read" your audience more completely and act, or react, accordingly.

It is essential to take this very seriously and to respect your audience fully. The empathy exercise shouldn't be facile or manipulative. It should be an honest effort to understand your audience so that you can address, to the best of your abilities, their circumstances, hopes, and dreams.

An excellent tool we use with our clients is the "Empathy Toy" created by our friends at 21 Toys (https://twentyonetoys.ca); we highly recommend you to take a look at what they do and how they do it.

The Online World

Just as it is in the world of face-to-face communication, the key to success when it comes to online communications is preparation. There is nothing more frustrating than finding yourself in the middle of an event, whether face-to-face or online, and suddenly having to deal with something that has gone wrong. Preparation is the key to minimizing that eventuality.

When preparing for an online event, there are four areas you must attend to:

1. **Pre-meeting communication with your guests to give them time to prepare.**

    1.1 **Clearly state the session's objectives** and ensure that all participants understand what part they will play in achieving those objectives.

    1.2 **Send an agenda** to all the meeting participants.

    1.3 **Netiquette.** Detail the meeting protocols and elicit agreement regarding the interaction between participants and maintaining mutual respect.

    1.4 **A list of required reference materials** should be sent to all attendees, making it clear who is responsible for each piece of material.

    1.5 **If the meeting is to be recorded**, be sure to inform the participants. This is a matter of common courtesy and, in many jurisdictions, it is the law.

1.6 If possible, pre-arrange to **have a co-facilitator**, to help you manage questions, deal with technical issues, and pitch in if you need to rest or are called away momentarily.

2. Your Equipment

2.1 We strongly recommend that you **use a headset with a boom microphone**, rather than your computer's microphone and speakers. This ensures that your microphone is always the same distance from your mouth.

2.2 If possible, use a **wired headset**. By doing this, you will remove the possibility that the batteries in your headset could run out in the middle of your session.

2.3 **Check your microphone** and acquaint yourself with its controls and settings to make sure you can be heard and understood during your meeting. For example, make sure your voice is being picked up by your headset's microphone, not your camera's microphone.

2.4 **Check your camera's field of view**, so that you know what the people you are speaking with can see in your surroundings.

2.5 Make sure your meeting **software** is capable of handling the length of your session and the number of participants that you are expecting to attend.

2.6 Familiarize yourself with the **features and idiosyncrasies** of your web conferencing software (polling, non-verbal interaction, chat, etcetera).

2.7 Be sure to **update your communications software**; developers frequently improve their applications.

2.8 **Have a complete backup** of all the equipment you will need to conduct your virtual session and practice changing equipment so that you can do it quickly.

2.9 **Be aware of your chair**. Chairs can be squeaky, wobble, or roll out of frame, etcetera.

2.10 If possible, **have a monitoring system** so you can see what the participants are seeing. This could be a second device that you log into as a participant. *Note*: remember to mute the microphone and speakers of the second device to avoid echo or feedback.

2.11 Before beginning your session, **check that everything you need is at hand** and working, including ancillaries such as pen, paper, resource materials, a glass of water, etcetera.

3. Your Environment

3.1 Everything your audience can see on their screen is important, including you, everything around you, and everything in **the background**. Treat your background as if was the backdrop on a stage. Ensure that it does not distract from what you are saying or the message you hope to share with the audience. Common examples of this are: readable book titles (unless you are promoting your book), distracting art or curios (unless you are promoting your art or curios), personal items that you'd prefer to not be made public, etcetera.

3.2 **Avoid backlights**. Sitting with a window or overly bright lamp behind you can turn you into a silhouette and leave your facial features in the shadows. If people can't see you, they can't connect with you.

3.3 **Have adequate and evenly distributed lighting**, not so dark you can't be seen, and not so bright it makes your eyes glow.

3.4 **Virtual backgrounds**, unless they are done very well, can be very distracting to an audience because they tend to create weird effects such as a melding of the speaker's hair or other body parts into the virtual background. To create an effective virtual background, you need a green screen, good lighting, and appropriate clothing. For this reason, we suggest sticking with a simple, clean, non-distracting background.

3.5 **Set your camera at eye level** so that you are looking straight into the lens in a natural, conversational way. Setting your camera too low (a laptop on a table) or too high (a camera set on top of a large monitor) may make you look unappealing and disconnected from your audience.

3.6 Life can be very noisy. Before you start your presentation, do your best to **minimize interior noise** around you (kids, pets, televisions, telephones). Nothing reduces the air of professionalism more than the sounds of a busy household.

3.7 **Environmental noise** is a more difficult problem to solve. Before beginning your session, assess the level of external noise (such as traffic or construction) and, if necessary, close the windows and doors of the room you are operating from. There are other sources of environmental noise that are more subtle and difficult to eliminate, such as the humming of an appliance; if you can turn it off, do so.

3.8 If **room echo** is the issue, consider hanging sound-absorbing materials such as art, curtains, or textile-based wall hangings.

4. Your Resources

Have all your **reference materials** and your agenda ready for the meeting and close at hand. The screen is your stage and, just as you never want to leave the stage during face-to-face meetings or presentations, you don't want to have to leave the screen to fetch materials out of your reach.

Case Study: Know your Audience

It was contract negotiation time between the provincial government and their unionized Professional Engineers. Jim was a negotiator for the union working to improve the situation for the union's members. In particular, the Land Surveyors group felt their compensation was no longer commensurate with the changes that had taken place in the industry and the more complex duties they were being asked to perform. When we first spoke with Jim, the union's presentation focused on the wants and needs of the surveyors and attempting to convey those wants and needs to negotiators representing the government's position.

At Sliding.ca one of the first questions we ask a presenter is "who is your audience?" Then, we ask "what does your audience want?" In this particular situation, the government negotiators had to satisfy the elected officials they were representing. After a brainstorming session, we felt we had a fairly solid idea of what the government negotiators wanted to accomplish in order to satisfy their superiors. Then, we moved on to the next question. What do the government negotiators not want? We came up with a set of ideas regarding what we could use to both positively and negatively motivate the audience.

Once we believed we had those answers we prepared a presentation that framed the requests of the Land Surveyors in language the government negotiators would understand, and that would also run parallel to their own wants and needs. After the union made its presentation using the approach we had created, the Land Surveyors not only got the percentage raise they were initially expecting, over the next three years they got 9% more wages than what the rest of the union members got.

Knowing and understanding your audience pays off.

Points to Consider

- Preparation is key to a successful presentation.
- Why this audience? Why now? Why here? Why should they listen to me?
- When presenting to an audience, always consider what is in it for them (WIIFT).
- Every time you show your presentation you should adapt to the circumstances surrounding that particular event.
- Make sure all the goals and objectives for your presentation are SMART.
- Always endeavour to be of benefit to your audience.
- Be empathetic.

Now that you have decided why you are presenting, and why you are presenting to this particular group of people, it is time to start creating your message and building your presentation.

In Chapter 3 we are going to share key elements we use to build a winning presentation.

3. CONTENT

Patrick Goes to the Movies

I came to Canada from Ireland when I was four-and-a-half years old. The year was 1957 and, up to that time, I hadn't seen any television shows and very few movies. Then, during my first year in Canada my mother took me to see Bambi. I don't remember anything about the theatre, but the movie itself has stuck with me ever since: the colour, characters, sound, and, of course, the storyline.

The movie is based on a book called "Bambi, a Life in the Woods," by Austrian author, Felix Salten, and the plot is pretty straightforward. A mule deer is born to a doe and a stag, he makes a few friends, makes a few silly mistakes, faces tragedy, grows up, enters a relationship, and reaches maturity. A simple story, to be sure; but a story that, when it was added to the National Film Registry of the Library of Congress, was cited as being "culturally, historically, and aesthetically significant." What made it so?

For me, the key to Bambi's great success and appeal is its simplicity and the universal journey that it took me on. I believe the same general truths expressed in Bambi apply to my life now as they did when I first experienced the joy of sitting with my mother watching it.

At Sliding.ca, each and every time we are tasked with creating a presentation for a client, or helping a client to create a presentation,

I think back to Bambi. I use it as a sort of 'back to basics' head clearing exercise, walking through the same steps that I can imagine a director going through in virtually every movie I've seen over the past many years.

- What is the movie (presentation) about? Bambi, is the story of a young deer growing up in the forest.

- What message is the director (presenter) hoping to share? The lesson to learn in Bambi is that life has its ups and downs but, if you never give up, eventually you will fulfill your destiny.

- What did the director (presenter) hope to accomplish? In Bambi the director hoped to entertain and inspire the audience.

- What is the metaphor in the movie (presentation)? In Bambi the movie is a metaphor for life, from birth to the realization of one's destiny.

- What journey did the director (presenter) take the audience on? From birth to adulthood, Bambi is the journey of life for a deer in the forest and, metaphorically, for every audience member in the theatre.

- What medium did the director (presenter) choose to use? Disney chose the medium of animation. In this way difficult topics could be tackled in a way that would be less jarring for a young audience.

- What would the film (presentation) look like? In Bambi, Disney chose to use a soft palette filled with gentle, pastel colours. As I look back, I can't imagine Bambi any other way.

A presentation should take the audience somewhere. Just as Disney took us on the journey of life in Bambi, our presentation should take our audience from where they are to where we'd like them to be.

Considering the fact that I am an inveterate movie buff, it is not surprising that I approach a presentation as though it were a movie script. I want to tell my audience a story, take them on a journey, keep them entertained along the way and, ultimately, move them to a better place. The same principles apply to a presentation.

Every time we climb onto a stage our goal is to deliver a message our audience will listen to, remember, and, hopefully, embrace. Unfortunately, far too often, speakers devote all their attention to the "listen" portion of that trio and ignore the "remember" portion. The "embrace" portion then becomes moot because it is impossible to embrace and act upon a message you can't remember.

At Sliding.ca we use a memorability scale to judge the effectiveness of a presentation:

1. Is the presenter's message clear, concise and compelling at the moment it is being delivered?

2. When surveyed, did members of the audience remember the presenter's main message one week after the presentation?

3. When surveyed, did members of the audience remember the presenter's main message three months after the presentation?

When you can ask somebody about a presentation they attended long ago and they can tell you what the main message was you know you've got an effective presentation.

Now it is time to talk about the three elements (The Triangle) required to communicate a message that your audience will listen to, remember long after they have left the venue and, hopefully, embrace and act upon.

3.1 The Triangle

Narrative, Design and Delivery

Every presentation, regardless of its type (slide show, speech, etcetera), has three components: narrative, design, and delivery. Let's look at the three components.

Narrative is the structure of the speech or presentation and includes an introduction, supporting points, and a close. The main idea of the narrative is that it must support your message, and it has to be entertaining and follow a storyline.

In our experience, for a narrative to be entertaining, it has to follow a story-line structure that will create ups and downs or problems and solutions, thus creating a clear contrast between before and after.

Design refers not only to the visual components (colour scheme, fonts, margins, images) in your presentation but also the words you will be using, the metaphor for your presentation, and the magical beat(s) created for your event.

Delivery is not only you speaking in front of an audience, it also has three parts: the environment, your voice, and your visual persona.

- Environment is everything related to the room you are presenting in, such as: visibility, sound characteristics, room temperature, and amenities. With regard to visibility, make sure the room is not too bright to allow for a clear view of your visual aids, check for blind spots, and try to eliminate any visual distractions. For sound characteristics, listen for distracting sources of noise on the stage and throughout the room. Room temperature can really affect the receptivity of your audience and should be controlled when possible. Last, but not least, assess the amenities in the room: Are the seats comfortable? Are there writing surfaces as needed? Is the general setup suited to the presentation you are about to make?

- Voice has different aspects that you should be aware of and try to master in order to become a proficient presenter. Learn to be aware of your volume, intonation, pace, use of pauses, etcetera.

- Visual persona includes the way you dress for the occasion, the use of the stage, your eye contact with the audience, and the way you use your arms and your entire body to help convey your message as effectively as possible.

We will talk about all the elements of delivery in much more depth in a later chapter of the book.

3.2 Create your Message...

...In One Succinct Sentence

Establishing the main message is very often the most difficult part of the creative process. When we sit down with a client one of the first things we ask them is "What do you want to say?" It's not unusual for the client to then spend thirty or forty minutes explaining to us what it is they want to share with their audience. We then ask them to put everything they have spent forty minutes explaining into one sentence.

This may seem like an impossible task, but it is absolutely necessary. Sharing ideas is hard; listening to, processing, and comprehending ideas is also hard. When you stand before an audience you have to do everything in your power to make it as easy as possible for them to deal with the information you are presenting. Having a main message makes it a lot easier to do this. The main message encapsulates that one vital piece of information that the audience must hear and understand. It constitutes the essence of the entire presentation and every point you make must explain, support, and further that message.

You may have heard of the elevator pitch. The elevator pitch is a scenario in which you get on an elevator and find yourself face to face with that one person you have been hoping to meet who can help you to advance your idea or project. The catch is that they are rushing to a meeting a few floors up and can only spare fifteen to twenty seconds for you to tell them what your project is all about. The point of the elevator pitch is that it forces you to distill your message into a form that is clear, concise, and compelling. The elevator pitch is the perfect tool to use to craft your main message.

Establishing a clear, concise, compelling main message for your presentation brings with it many advantages.

For example, when you are delivering your presentation, you might think of your main message as a lighthouse. The lighthouse is there to keep you on course and also to make sure you don't go astray and run aground upon the rocks of irrelevant information.

A clear, concise, and compelling main message is also much easier to repeat, and as we know, the key to successful advertising is repetition. By repeating your main message throughout your presentation, you will increase your audience's exposure to it, and make it more likely that they will remember it.

There's a lot going on during a presentation. Your audience is subject to a host of distractions, or ideas that they may find difficult to process or accept. By staying focused on the main message, you increase the chances that the audience will leave with your message firmly established in their memory and, hopefully, their hearts.

The main message is independent of the type and subtype of your presentation.

3.3 Types and Sub-types of Presentations

Inspire, Inform, Entertain, or Persuade

As we mentioned in chapter one, presenters often say that they present for one of four reasons: to inform, to entertain, to persuade, or to inspire. Most people, in fact, present for a combination of these reasons.

For the greater part of the 20th century practically every speech belonged to one of these four types. However, as the 21st century unfolds, the sources of information and stimuli we are exposed to are growing exponentially. Ironically, to manage the overwhelming amount of data we are bombarded by, we all too often retreat into communities of common thought, people that think like us and share the same ideas as us. Unfortunately, this can result in a constant reaffirmation of our own ideas and a comfortable avoidance of any ideas we find challenging. In our opinion, this is the most intriguing paradox we face in this age of information.

In order to overcome this vexing problem, and to make sure your presentation is effective and memorable, we recommend that you stop trying to overtly persuade your audience and eliminate that type of speech from your repertoire. Instead, use varying combinations of the remaining types of presentations and concentrate on informing, entertaining, and inspiring your audience.

In order to effectively combine different types of presentations we suggest adopting the concept of the speech or presentation "subtype." To do this, begin by deciding on a primary presentation type and then choose a secondary type that supports and reinforces the primary. For example, if you have information you need to share, try to inspire your audience to embrace the information rather than just sharing it with them.

An informative and inspiring presentation has as its main objective to convey information. By inspiring the audience to embrace that information, the effectiveness of the presentation will be greatly enhanced. Conversely, an inspiring and informative presentation intends to inspire your audience to take action supported with pertinent information.

Note: Audiences can be hard to entertain, so don't be surprised if the majority of your presentations and speeches fall into the inform-inspire or inspire-inform categories.

Being aware of the hierarchy of the types and sub-types you are employing will greatly enhance your chances of being effective and successful.

3.4 Discover the Metaphor

A Metaphor is Worth a Thousand Pictures

The Oxford Dictionary provides two definitions for the word metaphor:

1. A metaphor is a figure of speech in which a word or phrase is applied to an object or action to which it is not literally applicable.

2. A metaphor is a word or phrase used to be representative or symbolic of something else.

William Shakespeare created one of history's most famous metaphors when, in 1599, he wrote the following phrase for his play *As You Like It*. "All the world's a stage, and all the men and women merely players."

In this metaphor Shakespeare is not literally saying that the world is a stage. Rather, he is using the image of a stage to symbolize our existence and the image of players, or actors, to symbolize the different faces we present to each other.

Another wonderful metaphor is the phrase "Conscience is a man's compass," coined by Vincent Van Gogh. It's a simple little phrase but the image it creates tells us exactly what Van Gogh was trying to say. It also does so in a way that conjures up an image that provides the stepping stone that allows the listener to conjure up further images associated with direction, or travel, or a journey, etcetera. That simple little phrase provides a palette for the listener to paint an interpretation of Van Gogh's message in their mind that is in keeping with their own personal experience and view of the world.

This is the beauty of metaphors. So much of the interpretation of the symbolism lies in the imagination of the listener. A well-designed metaphor can help to simplify even the most complicated concepts or ideas and make them tangible for practically any audience.

By creating a metaphor that you can use to run through your presentation you will make it easier for your audience to follow your thought process. The metaphor will make your ideas more accessible to your audience and will help them remember you and your main message long after they have left the venue.

They say a picture is worth a thousand words. Well, metaphors help you to paint pictures in the mind of the listener. Those pictures, in turn, help you to move your narrative forward by, symbolically, showing the similarities between the message you want to present and the audience's personal experience.

In choosing the overlying metaphor for your presentation you should, once again, think about your audience and what you have learned about them. Previously, we used the example of the Calgary Stampede and standing before a group to speak about roping cattle wearing a chef's hat and carrying a spatula. Well, think of your metaphor in the same way. Ideally, you will want to select a metaphor that your audience will relate to and then use images to support the metaphor that the audience will recognize and take home with them.

Metaphors are powerful. They will breathe life into your words, they will make your main and supporting messages easier to understand and remember, and they will add color, pizzazz, and excitement to your presentations.

3.5 The Journey (Story)

Take Your Audience to a Better Place

Creating a presentation is like embarking on a journey. You start with an idea, then flesh it out and move through all the steps required to hone it and make it easy to understand and engaging for your audience.

As a presenter, you should try to take your audience on a journey and send them home changed from the way they walked in. Metaphorically, you want to take your audience to a better place.

That better place can take many forms. In a presentation meant to entertain it can take the form of an uplifting story, or a humorous tale, or a stimulating experience. In a presentation meant to inform it can manifest itself as the answer to a question, or the solution to a problem, or an introduction to a new idea. In a presentation meant to inspire it can be that emotional high we feel after hearing a compelling story. Regardless of the motivation these are all "better places."

Thinking of your presentation in terms of a journey will help you to infuse it with a sense of movement and progress which will lend itself to all kinds of metaphors. Even better, most of those metaphors are associated with solid, tangible images that can be used to paint amazing pictures for your audience.

The journey can be framed in terms of cars, or boats, or planes, or any other method of transportation you can envision. Or, the journey can move from one location to another, or from one time-frame to another. The journey can even move from one dimension to another; the possibilities are endless.

Taking your audience on a journey also makes it easier to present them with your call to action, the summons to "get on board" before the train leaves the station.

Your journey embodies everything you are trying to accomplish when you present. You are there to take people somewhere, to enlighten them, make them happy, lift them up and improve their lives in some small way.

By imagining yourself on an adventure as you create your presentation, and then imagining yourself taking your audience to that better place you make the goal tangible and easier to grasp for both you and your audience.

In addition to metaphors helping to clarify your message, metaphors also help to visualize the theme (motif) and mood of the presentation. For instance, a sailing metaphor might suggest the use of a blue colour palette and marine imagery. Imagine a financial planning presentation, featuring the metaphor of a retired couple, sailing to the destination of their dreams on a sapphire sea.

3.6 Paper first

Computers Engender Tunnel Vision

One of the biggest traps people fall into when creating a presentation is to start creating it right on their computer. Most people usually do this to save time. The thought process is: "If my presentation is going to end up as a PowerPoint file, why not start working on that file right away." This perceived notion of efficiency blurs your view of the elements of your presentation, greatly hampering its effectiveness. According to the Oxford Dictionary, effectiveness is: "The degree to which something is successful in producing a desired result," while efficiency means: "Achieving maximum productivity with minimum wasted effort or expense." While it is always nice to do everything as efficiently as possible, in our experience, when it comes to presentations, effectiveness is far more important than efficiency. Once you master the art of creating effective presentations, efficiency will follow. We call this the efficiency paradox.

In addition to the possibility of surrendering effectiveness for efficiency, there are, at least three more disadvantages resulting from starting work on your presentation on your computer.

First, by starting your work on presentation software you ignore one of the first important planning questions you have to ask: Do I even need a slide deck to convey my message effectively? In our interactions with clients, we routinely hear about the bad presentations given in boardrooms and how many presenters "hide" behind their slide deck. We've even heard stories in which PowerPoint has been actually banned from the boardroom[ix]. As much as we can appreciate the frustration people feel after sitting through their umpteenth bad presentation, banning the format is overly simplistic, solves nothing, and only serves to deprive the presenter of a very useful tool.

Second, by its very nature presentation software operates in a linear fashion. This is all well and good, however, the consequence of beginning your work on a linear tool, such as PowerPoint, is the loss of perspective. This robs you of the ability to see other, perhaps better, more innovative or attractive possibilities. In a way, it is the same as working with mind-maps, which are much richer, than simply using lists.

Third, the effect of starting your work directly on the computer is that the different stages in the creation of a presentation (planning, design, delivery) can get blurred. Dividing the work into distinctive stages helps you to concentrate on one stage at a time and to deal with the requirements of each stage separately. This results in a more logical and effective workflow and, as a consequence, your audience will be more likely to act based on your message.

That is why we suggest you start the creative process away from your computer. More specifically, the planning stage should be done on paper in the most creative way possible: using crayons, markers, coloured pencils, and plain or coloured stock in odd shapes (like a circle or a square). To get the most out of this process, try to avoid using typical 8.5" x 11" vertical sheets. Something we have tried with great success, particularly when brainstorming with groups, is the use of large sheets of square paper (start with 11" x 17" and trim the excess to make it square). We then place the square on the table among the participants and ask them to brainstorm by writing three-word phrases or drawing images that represent the ideas they are trying to flesh out. In order to banish linear thought from the process, we turn the page 90° at regular intervals. We have even gone so far as to give crayons to the participants, rather than pens and pencils. To continue with the creative process, we then recommend the transfer of the brainstorm or mind-map ideas to sticky notes, which we will detail in the next section.

3.6.1 Sticky Notes

They Add Flexibility to the Process and Help You to Break Down Ideas

In our effort to escape the trap of linear thinking that is often imposed by presentation software, and the illusion of efficiency discussed in the last section, we suggest the use of sticky notes. It is one of the best ways to continue the creative process on paper. Sticky notes provide great flexibility and bring a fresh perspective to the process (modularity and malleability). They provide at least three advantages:

First. They will give you the flexibility to, literally, move the different elements of your presentation in order to help you find the best sequencing and optimal grouping. Using sticky notes also makes it easier to find and eliminate unnecessary information. This will help you to convey your message more effectively and minimize the possibility of overwhelming your audience.

Second. Sticky notes are magnificently mobile. You can, for instance, have a brainstorming session with your team in a boardroom using a whiteboard and then take them with you on a piece of Bristol board or in your journal.

Third. By far the most important advantage of using sticky notes is the change in perspective or point of view it brings you. In a way, it's like turning your presentation into a modular and malleable sculpture that you can view from different angles and change at will. This will allow you to see "hidden" or unexpected aspects of your presentation and reveal other ways to organize your information.

In addition to these advantages, the changes you make are all easily undone in case the path you are exploring at any given time is not working. Furthermore, this will encourage you and your team to explore other possibilities and free you from preconceived, cookie-cutter ideas that generally result in boring, uninspiring, and forgettable presentations.

We also recommend you take advantage of the contrasting colours which you can get in sticky notes. Use different colours to separate the different elements in your presentation. For instance, you could use one colour for section titles, another colour for content, a third colour for the graphic drafts of your slides, a fourth colour for notes, etcetera. Just be sure to keep your colour coding consistent in order to avoid confusion.

One key and crucial requirement in using sticky notes effectively is to write or draw no more than one idea per note. This will ensure that you won't end up with competing ideas or messages in your slides. And, when the concept you are trying to convey is complex, keep in mind that you can use more than one sticky note to communicate that complicated idea. We strongly suggest the use of sticky notes.

 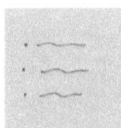 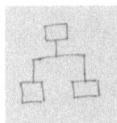  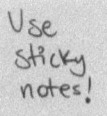

In the interest of simplicity, we would also like to suggest the use of markers or crayons to write or draw on your sticky notes. This will force you to reduce the amount of information that you will be able to put in a single note and it will help you to free your mind. Additionally, it's easier when working in a team environment because your writing will be visible to all the members of the group. When working in this type of environment we take a picture of the sticky notes to create a reference that we can then send to every member of the team. And, best of all, using markers or crayons makes the picture more readable and more fun to look at.

3.7 Medium

"The Medium is the Message,"
...and Environment ...and Resources

The medium is the means by which something is communicated or expressed. Simply put, it is the collection of ways in which your audience receives your information. These ways are, essentially, the five senses most humans have at their disposal.

While most presentations use both visual and verbal media, this is not always the case. You may be doing a presentation on wine or coffee tasting, which will give you a rare opportunity to address two more of our senses (media): taste and smell. The sensorial experience might even be expanded to include touch, say, if you were introducing a new type of stemware designed to enhance the wine tasting experience.

That said, sometimes you will only engage one of the senses. For example, if you are doing a slide presentation for a kiosk, you may not need sound. You could also be working on a presentation for a visually impaired audience or working on the auditory aid for such an audience. However, for the purposes of this book, we will focus on traditional presentations that encompass both visual and auditory components. In this chapter, we will deal with the visual; the auditory medium will be discussed in Chapter 4.

Visual aids will help you to convey your message in a memorable way. Those aids can include slides, flip-charts, whiteboards, and often, nothing. Yes, nothing. Nothing but your presence, your voice, and your message. One of the first questions we ask our clients when we are coaching, or designing a presentation for them, is whether they even need a visual aid. Our initial suggestion is almost always… "use nothing." As we move through our coaching process this is the first exercise we use as we search for the most effective way for the client to convey their message. The idea is to start the process of constructing your presentation with as open a mind as possible. We encourage you to try to see and explore all the possibilities available to you before even starting your presentation.

As we mentioned previously, many presenters' first impulse is to move straight to slide presentation software and, even though we commonly do end up using it, it is not where we want to begin. We believe that questioning the true effectiveness and utility of a slide deck, or of any medium for that matter, is a great exercise for deciding upon the most effective medium for your presentation.

Always try to use the medium that best suits your message, environment, and resources. Sometimes it is difficult, but you should always try to fight external pressure and your own inertia when selecting the best visual medium for your presentation.

With that in mind, let's now discuss the peculiarities and best practices for each of the visual mediums available to us. As Marshall McLuhan said, "The medium is the message[x]."

3.7.1 Slides, Flip Chart, White Board, or Speech

Your Tool Must Fit the Need

These days most presentations incorporate the use of a slide deck (PowerPoint, Keynote, Prezi, etcetera). As ubiquitous as slide decks may be, you should always consider the potential benefits of using a flip-chart, a white board, or a speech (without visual aids).

Slide presentations offer many advantages, such as big projection size, multimedia capabilities, and the power to use animations to explain complex concepts and processes (used tastefully and in the proper measure). Despite these advantages, a slide deck might not be the best option for conveying your message. Consequently, it is important to choose the tool that best suits your message, your audience, and the environment in which you will be delivering your presentation.

Slide decks are particularly well suited for presentations to larger audiences. If you have a small audience of about 20 people or less, consider using a flip chart, a white board, or a combination of both, keeping in mind that these tools have a limitation in size and an inherent inability to incorporate multimedia. Because of these characteristics, flip charts and white boards are better suited to cozier environments. This increased level of intimacy should also promote more spontaneity, interaction, and connection with your audience.

Besides the size of your audience, you should also consider the expectations and preconceptions of your public. In certain circles and occasions, a slide presentation is seen as the standard way to conduct your presentation and a flip chart or a white board could be seen as amateurish or unprofessional. Nevertheless, even in these circumstances, a well-planned and masterfully executed flip chart presentation could help you to stand out from your competition.

Whichever tool that you consider best for the job, always do these three things:

1. Carefully plan the contents of your slides, flip chart, or white board. For example: on a flip chart, trace the contents of every page (text, diagrams, etc.) with a thin pencil line, so that only you can see it; then, during the presentation, draw on top of the thin pencil line with markers.

2. Be prepared! For example: always check that you have the right kind of markers (it's really embarrassing to leave your

"indelible mark" on a customer's white board) and that they are in good shape, bring extra paper in case you need to continue the conversation, consider using a flip-chart as a backup for your projector, etcetera.

3. Practice, practice, practice, and then, practice a bit more.

Tool	Best for...	Avoid when...
Slide Show	– any size audience – presenting data – multimedia – explaining complex concepts or processes	– audience perceives slide decks as boring – use could hamper connection with your audience
Flip Charts and White Boards	– small to medium audiences – explaining simple concepts or processes – enhancing your connection with the audience	– concepts or processes are complex – presenting data. – audiences perceive them as unprofessional.
Speech	– any size audience – enhancing your connection with the audience – storytelling	– visual explanations are needed – multimedia is required

If you don't have to present data or explain a concept or process that requires a visual explanation, delivering a speech (without visual aids) is often a powerful and refreshing option. In section 4 we will talk about how to deliver a completely verbal presentation.

3.7.2 Prioritizing

Every Audience Has its Limit

A major problem with many presentations is that they convey too much information for most people to absorb effectively in one session. On top of the information you are providing them during your presentation, consider the volume of stimuli they are being subjected to on a daily basis and the limited amount of information that the human brain can process in short periods of time.

In order to keep your audience awake and interested, and also to provide them with additional information that they can go through at a later date, a great tool to use is the handout.

Nowadays, the handout has become an underutilized tool. However, in the old days, before PowerPoint, it was an essential part of a standard presentation. Because of the very limited amount of information that one could put on a 35mm slide, we were forced to supplement our on-screen information with added information in the form of a handout.

Then, presentation software came along[xi]. Presentation software made it easier, often to the detriment of the presentation, to put a lot of information onto every slide. To make things worse, it also made it easier to print out slides as a handout. This creates a two-fold problem. First, most audience members' brains are overwhelmed when the slides they are presented with contain too much information. Second, most handouts (when they are provided) are merely a regurgitation of the information already provided by the presenter, rather than a useful tool designed to increase the understanding of the presenter's message.

In hindsight, we now know that the limitations imposed by 35 mm slides, turned out to be a positive thing. By limiting the amount of information conveyed to the audience, we greatly increase the likelihood that they will understand and remember our message. Simultaneously, the handout served as the perfect vehicle for providing any extra information that still needed to be passed along. This greatly increased the memorability of the presentation. The reason for this is that the human brain retains information for much longer when it is provided in short bursts, with a time separation in between the bursts, rather than when information is provided in a large dump all at once (Medina).

What we end up with is a conflict between the amount of information that people can absorb in a short period of time and the amount of information that needs to be passed along to the audience. At Sliding.ca we believe that the best way to solve this problem is through the use of a well-designed handout.

When constructing a presentation, the first question we ask is: what information are we going to put on our slides, flip-chart, or white board? The second question is: what information are we going to leave out or provide to the audience in a handout? To get the answers to these questions, we prioritize our information using the following scale:

A. what the audience **must** know

B. what the audience **should** know

C. what the audience **may like** to know

Then, as we build our presentation:

A. goes onto your slide deck, flip-chart, or white board

B. goes into your handout

C. could be mentioned in passing, saved for Q&A, or shared later

The process of prioritizing and separating your information should be performed before you start working on your presentation software, flip chart pages, or white board.

3.7.3 Create a Handout

Hey… Who Doesn't Like a Handout?

Besides a handout being very effective in supporting a simplified slide deck, it will also help you to continue the conversation after your presentation has been delivered and can be distributed in hard copy or electronically.

Following the prioritizing method defined previously, we decide what to include in a handout by following the same hierarchy (**A** - what the audience must know, **B** - what the audience should know, **C** - what the audience may like to know).

Put only **A** materials on your slides, put **B** materials on your handouts, and leave your **C** materials as information to discuss when you reconnect with them at a later date or time.

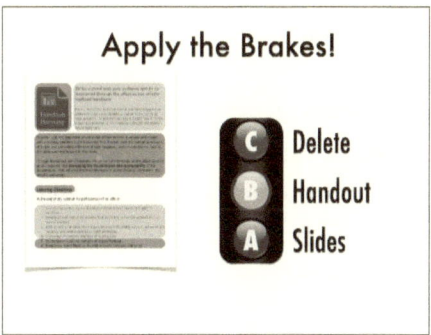

Your final handout will contain:

A. A thumbnail of the slide, **A**

B. Printed or digital information that your audience should know, **B**

C. None of **C**

Surprisingly, the tool to create effective handouts has been hidden under our noses in PowerPoint (or whatever presentation software you happen to use). The "secret" consists in using the **Notes Page View** to create your handout.

The **Handouts View** can then be used to print your presentation guide/notes.

Very often, to create handouts, presenters use, either, the Handouts View or they just print their slides. This is not an effective practice because it merely reproduces overloaded slides.

Using the **Notes Page** to create your handouts allows you to show your key information separately, in area **A**, in a way that is easy for the audience to absorb, understand, and remember. This will leave you free to write other important, but not key, information in area **B** (the presentation software's notes area).

The **Notes Page** will automatically place an image of the slide, area **A**, on the page for you. This serves as a handy reference for your audience, so that they can landmark where the information is on the handouts. As a bonus, you will be able to see the information in area **B** in the Presenters Screen during your presentation.

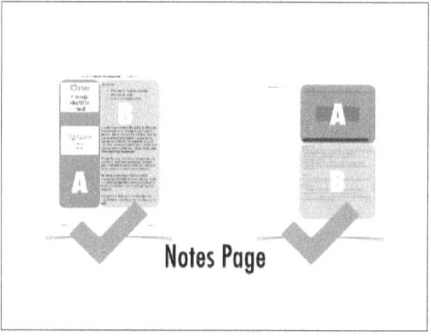

For example, the slide below is ineffective because it is showing too much information (**A** + **B**). This dilutes the slide's main message, which is "75% of all food poisoning cases start in the kitchen" (**A**).

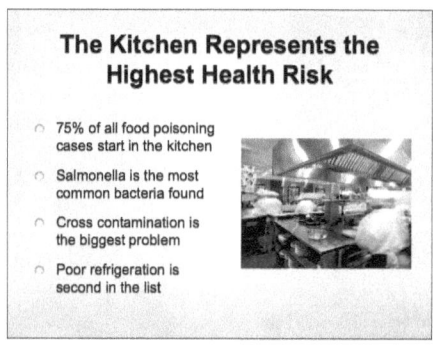

By leaving only **A** as the information on the slide you maximize impact and memorability. This leaves the audience with a clear and strong message and makes it easier for them to remember and absorb.

However, as we discussed earlier, **B** may also consist of important information. Unfortunately, your audience only has a limited amount of time to absorb the information on a slide. When you consider the difficulty audiences have reading small text, including information labeled as **B** will force you to reduce the text size, making it hard to read. For these reasons, it makes much better sense to save the **B** information for a handout. Voilà!

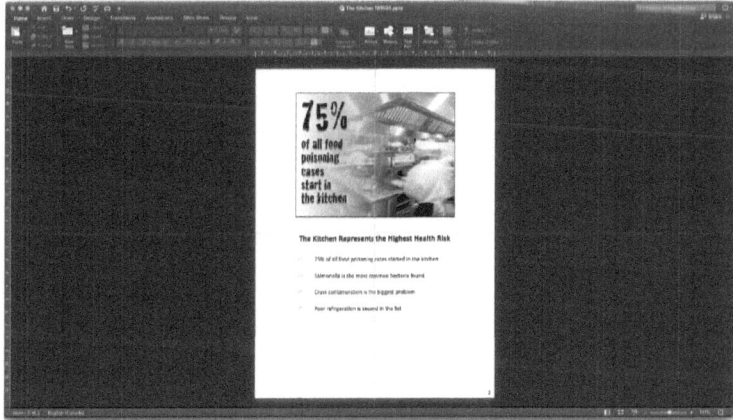

3.8 Design Principles

"Be So Good They Can't Ignore You" —Steve Martin

Design principles are a set of agreed upon rules, guidelines, and advice, that presenters drawn upon in order to make information more attractive, organized, and comprehensible for the viewer.

Let's start with slide deck content.

3.8.1 Slide Deck Content

Clear, Concise, and Compelling

In order for your message to be relevant and memorable it must be easy to understand, simply stated, and emotionally powerful. At Sliding.ca we use the adjectives: "Clear, concise, and compelling" to describe our ideal presentation. We then strive to eliminate or, at least, minimize anything that gets in the way of achieving that ideal. For most presenters, the "compelling" portion of this triad is self-evident, it is the "clear" or the "concise" portions that pose the problem.

When we present, we are motivated by a desire to fully explain our message. The problem arises when, in an effort to achieve that goal, we end up over-explaining or putting so much information on the screen that the message gets lost or fuzzy and nothing causes an audience to tune out faster than ambiguity. When creating content for your slide deck it is important to keep in mind that the information on the screen is there to punctuate and enhance what you have said. Always remember, you are the message, the slide deck is there to provide you with support and reinforcement.

As you prepare content for your slide deck be strict in your editing process. If an image or piece of information doesn't contribute to and fully support your main message, delete it. As we say at Sliding.ca: "When in doubt, leave it out."

Keep in mind that your slide deck is not only there to support your message but also to support the journey you are taking your audience on. Try to ensure that there is a coherence and flow to the images and information you provide; one way to accomplish this goal is by sticking to your metaphor. You should also endeavour to maintain a consistent motif in your presentation.

3.8.2 Your Main Message

"You Must Remember This..."

Advertising works! That's why companies and advertisers spend huge amounts of money coming up with catchy mottos or catch phrases with which to promote their products or services.

The more times a consumer sees or hears a company's catchphrase the more memorable it will become and the more engrained it will become in the consumer's psyche. Nike: "Just Do It," BMW: "The Ultimate Driving Machine," M&M: "Melts in Your Mouth, Not in Your Hands," Bounty Towels: "The Quicker Picker Upper," Lay's: "Betcha Can't Eat Just One." Ideally, by the time you have completed your presentation, your main message will also be ingrained in your "consumer's" psyche.

So, how do you increase the chances that your audience will remember your main message long after they leave the venue? By making that message clear, concise, and compelling, and then placing it within an environment (your words, your slide deck, your venue, your pre and post presentation interaction with your audience, etcetera) that supports it fully and constantly reinforces it.

Every time you stand and deliver a presentation you are, essentially, endeavouring to sell your ideas to your audience. The idea you are advocating for is your product and your main message is your catchphrase. A well-constructed main message, or catchphrase, is the most powerful tool you will use to sell that product. Remember: advertising works.

3.8.3 Bite-Size Slides

Info Snacks

One of the most vexing limitations you have to address when designing a slide deck is that all the members of your audience are human. As humans, we are limited in our capacity to understand, process, and recall information (Medina).

Among other things, one of the most effective ways to address this inherent limitation is to show the audience only one idea per slide. By showing only one idea per slide, you give the human brain the opportunity to process information quickly and efficiently.

Every time you find yourself combining more than one message on a slide, even if they are complementary, it is time to introduce the Bite-Size Slide rule and give each idea its own slide.

By following this rule, you will have a clearer message without distractions. As an added benefit you will also create cleaner slides that are easier for your audience to understand, process, and recall.

If you have a complex message, you may have to break it down into even more than one slide.

One common obstacle to the application of this rule is that, in some environments (like when you have to pitch an idea to a venture capitalist) you may be limited to a specific number of slides. If you need to present complex ideas that might require more than the dictated number of slides, conveying your message becomes that much more complicated.

To overcome this dilemma, we propose using what we like to call the "virtual slide." Virtual slides are created using animations. We define a virtual slide as a group of animations that run automatically, either in combination or individually, initiated by a single click.

For example, let's say you want to show a map of Canada with all of the provinces appearing individually, one after the other, from east to west. But, you also want to stop at Ontario so that you can focus on it before showing the rest of the provinces. You could animate the slides so that the Atlantic provinces appeared one after the other, from Newfoundland moving west to Quebec, on a single click. You could then have Ontario appear on a second single click. After speaking about Ontario, you could then initiate the appearance of the remaining provinces, one after the other from Manitoba westward, on a third click.

With the intelligent and measured use of animations, not only will you overcome the problem of being limited to a specific number of slides, you will also find that your slides are more dynamic, and that your audience is more entertained and attentive. We will talk more about animations later in this chapter.

3.8.4 One Motif

Polka Dots and Stripes... Really?

A dominant or recurring idea in an artistic work is called a motif. In other words, a motif is the collection of visual elements in your presentation, such as fonts, colours, graphic elements, and use of space.

All the elements in your presentation, whether visual or not, must complement each other and support and promote your main message.

When your motif is not crystal clear, or you have more than one motif, it sends an ambiguous message that distracts and confuses your audience and diminishes the effectiveness of your presentation.

Your motif must be established before you start working with presentation software. Once you have a first draft of your slides on sticky notes, take time to consciously and purposely define the motif of your presentation. Ask yourself: What are the best fonts to use in my presentation? What colours will best suit the style of my presentation? Which type of graphic elements will be in keeping with my choice of fonts and colours? How can I most effectively use the slide space available to me?

In our experience, the best guide to use when defining your motif will be your metaphor. For example, we previously used the image of a retired couple, sailing to the destination of their dreams on a sapphire sea. To support that metaphor, you could utilize the colour sapphire (or, a subtle blue colour scheme), images of sailing, and a font that suggests movement. By selecting those graphic elements (colours, images and fonts) you would create a motif that supports your metaphor, which would, in turn, support your main message.

Many times, these elements are dictated by the branding of your department or company. However, we have found that, very often, these templates offer too many options. If this is the case, we recommend using only a subset of the mandated options. Even when working with a mandated set of options you should still try to link your motif to your metaphor.

The initial slides in your presentation are very important because they will define your motif in the eyes of the audience. For instance, the first time you show a slide title will define how the rest of the slide titles in your presentation should look. If, in subsequent slides, you change any of these characteristics, you will introduce doubt or confusion in the minds of your audience and they will wonder, consciously or unconsciously, why those changes were made. As a hard and fast rule, the visual anchoring that occurs on these first slides, must be adhered to for all subsequent visual elements in your presentation.

Let's take a look at the different elements that define your motif.

3.8.4.1 Fonts

Keep it Simple

One or two font types in a couple of font sizes, and with one or two attributes (such as bold, light, or italic), will provide you with more than enough options for the different text elements of your slide deck without compromising the consistency of your design.

As with every other element of the design of your presentation, we recommend you exercise restraint. When you have too many fonts (more than two is too many) it can be confusing for your audience. Remember, every element of your presentation must support your message.

The key aspect to consider in selecting your typefaces and font sizes is readability[xii]. Make sure that your text is always large enough and clean enough to be easily read by everyone in the room. An additional advantage to using large text is that it will limit the number of words you can put on the screen, thus, helping you to keep your message clear and concise.

3.8.4.2 Colour

Simplicity is Elegance

When it comes to colour, it is just as important to exercise restraint. One, two, or three colours are enough for the vast majority of slide decks. Remember, the goal is to create a consistent design. To accomplish this, use the same colours for associated elements and select a colour palette that will support your message rather than distract from it. Colour sets the mood of a presentation and, like text, it is a powerful tool for conveying your message effectively. Base your colour decisions on your message and the makeup of your audience.

3.8.4.3 Images

Reinforce your Metaphor

In a world that seems to be more and more visually dominant, images are a great tool to help you convey your message. They can be used for many purposes: to conjure up an emotion, evoke a memory, illustrate a point, or to explain something that could be very difficult to explain with words.

Using images to enhance your presentation design

Consistency is one of the keys to attaining a polished look. Using a coherent set of images is as important as choosing the right font and a well-coordinated colour palette. For instance, you wouldn't mix clip art with photographs or illustrations.

When choosing photographs for your presentation consider:

1. Using pictures that show only what you are trying to say
2. Looking for images that work well with your colour palette
3. Avoiding the use of clichés

Say no to frames

When you are using one picture in a slide, make the most of it by filling the slide with the image. In effect, the image will become the background and you will avoid the "picture frame look," as depicted in this slide:

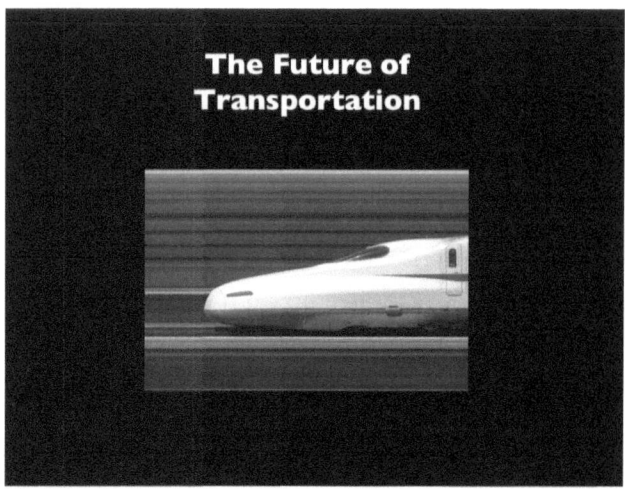

One of the biggest problems arises when images are resized. It is very common to see images that are crooked or stretched due to the use of an improper resizing technique. To avoid skewing an image or changing its aspect ratio when resizing it, always use the corners of the image to change its size.

> **Note**: When you need to crop or resize a photograph and you want to maintain the quality of the image it is important to use an image with dimensions that are larger than the slide.

Cultural considerations

In the western world, we read from left to right. Consequently, we perceive forward movement (whether in space or time) as moving from left to right. In some cultures, this perception may be reversed. Here's an example: the caption on the previous image talks about the future of transportation; however, in that image the train feels as though it is coming *from* the future rather than going *to* the future. In the following image, after the picture has been flipped horizontally, the train, correctly, feels as though it is moving towards the future.

3.8.4.4 Animations

> *"With Animation, Fantasy is Your Friend"*
> — Steven Spielberg

Used judiciously, animations provide a way of introducing sequential bits of information to your audience. You can also use them to show the steps in a process, or a change in distance, direction, or relationship.

When used wisely and elegantly, animations are a great tool for illustrating concepts and processes, and for guiding your audience through complex ideas. However, when animations are used excessively, or for no apparent reason, they can make your slide deck appear overly busy and dizzying. This can subject your audience to what we refer to as "The hiccup effect."

The key to an effective use of animations is to use them with a very clear purpose that supports your message and doesn't compete with it. People are naturally drawn to moving objects; when used improperly, animations can be very distracting.

Remember, with animations, you can create virtual slides.

The Online World

In an online environment, your audience has more immediate sources of distraction that, compounded with the anonymity intrinsic to the medium, could negatively impact the memorability of your message.

Once you go online, that back-and-forth exchange of eye contact and energy becomes minimized, and your 3D experience becomes a 2D experience.

When creating content for your online session, keep in mind:

- Screen sizes vary widely from palm-size to wall-size.

- You are competing with distractions that are immediate and can be highly engaging.

- You are limited in the amount of feedback you receive from your audience, making it more difficult to assess your audience's level of engagement.

- Anonymity greatly reduces the positive effects that peer pressure can have on an audience's behaviour.

When preparing content for a virtual event, there are several things to remember:

1. **Everything the camera sees is content**

    1.1 Before you begin your session, **check your face and hair** on camera to ensure you're comfortable with how you look.

1.2 Check your clothing and be sure to **dress appropriately** for the session you are beginning.

1.3 Scan the image on your screen to **see what your camera sees** and ensure it is not showing things that could be distracting or that the audience should not see.

2. Slide Content

2.1 In an online world, keeping your slides **uncluttered and clear** is crucial because your viewer may be watching the presentation on a small-screen device.

2.2 For the very same reason, it is also very important to **adhere to the Bite-Size Slide rule**.

2.3 As a bonus, using Bite-Size Slides will force you to **change slides more often**, which helps to maintain an audience's attention.

3. Animations and Transitions

3.1. Slide animations and transitions are excellent tools you can use to maintain your audience's attention by making them more dynamic and interesting to watch.

3.2. If you show all the slide content at once, the points you are trying to make may compete with each other. By using animations, you can **introduce every piece of information individually** (like a bullet point of a block on a diagram).

This will help you to control the data flow and make it easier for your audience to absorb.

Case Study: Massage your Metaphors

Alexis, was working on a presentation she was giving to a group of FileMaker developers in Las Vegas, Nevada. Our goal in working with Alexis was to make the technical content of her presentation as accessible, understandable, and entertaining to her audience as possible. The challenge was to come up with a metaphor that illustrated to her audience that designing was a process. To this end, we decided to compare the process of designing, to the process of going on a journey. The metaphor was an automobile taking a trip with stops along the way to reflect the various stages of the design process. Alexis' presentation took the audience on that journey from point to point. The presentation was visually pleasing, fun to look at, and made it possible for every point Alexis had to make to stand on its own while still remaining integrated into the whole. The audience loved Alexis' presentation. She has been asked back to present for FileMaker developers every year since then and still gets complimented on the effectiveness of that first presentation.

Metaphors make it easier for your audience to listen to, absorb, and remember your message.

Points to Consider

- Take your audience on a journey.

- Every successful presentation revolves around a clear, concise, and compelling main message that your audience MUST hear, understand, and remember.

- Metaphors make it easier for your audience to absorb your message.

- Start on paper, away from your computer, and use sticky notes to storyboard your presentation.

- Use the medium that best suits your message, environment, and resources.

- Use the ABC system to prioritize your content and decide what should be included in your slide deck (A), saved for your handout (B), or omitted (C).

- The sole purpose of your slide deck is to support your message.

- One idea per slide.

- Keep your slide deck design simple and consistent.

- Animations can help you explain complex concepts and processes.

Congratulations; you have a presentation. Now, it is time to present it to a real, live, breathing audience.

In Chapter 4 we will discuss what it takes to share a message in a way the audience will listen to, embrace, and remember long after you've left the stage.

Let's talk about delivery.

Inspire or Perish

4. DELIVERY

"There are Only Two Types of Speakers in the World, the Nervous and the Liars"

— Mark Twain

At Sliding.ca, we like to compare the delivery of a presentation or a speech to going on a first date. When you go on a first date, you're not entirely sure how you will be received. You hope you will enjoy each other's company and, regardless of whether you see each other again, you hope it will be a stimulating and enjoyable experience. Not unlike delivering a presentation or a speech.

When preparing for a night out it would be wise to pick a location that both you and your date feel comfortable in. If you were going out with someone who's a member of PETA (People for the Ethical Treatment of Animals), you probably wouldn't have much fun if you ended up going to a rodeo.

It would also be wise to dress appropriately. Ideally, your appearance would convey the message that you have respect for yourself and for your date.

On a date, it's important that you be able to comfortably and clearly communicate with each other so that you can discuss common interests or outlooks.

When we go out with somebody, we hope they will feel entertained by us. This doesn't mean we have to be "on" the whole evening, but it would be nice if they found us interesting and somewhat memorable. How wonderful it would be to go on a date and feel comfortable enough that we could share honest emotions and feelings with them.

This chapter will help you to approach your presentations with the skills and confidence that will allow you to stand before any audience, anywhere, anytime and, effectively, share your message.

Delivery matters! An audience will remember how they experienced your presentation just as much, if not more, than what was in your presentation.

Remember, every time you stand to deliver a message, whether it be one on one to a friend or colleague or to a group of a thousand people, you are competing with the enormous volume of stimuli vying for your audience's attention. Think about the number of times you've been in a movie theatre and saw someone paying more attention to their cell phone than the movie. The same thing is going on with your audience. The attention span of humans appears to be getting shorter and shorter (Medina). Consequently, it is becoming increasingly necessary to cut through the noise that distracts us.

In order to overcome this tsunami of competing stimuli you have to deliver something special, every time you present. To do this, you have to create an environment that supports your message and sends your audience home receptive to and embracing of your message.

Let's take a closer look at how to accomplish this.

4.1 Environment

"The Environment is Everything that isn't Me"
— Albert Einstein

Whenever you deliver a presentation every aspect of your environment contributes to the show and affects how you will deliver your message. Consequently, it's important to know as much about the venue you will be performing in as possible.

In an earlier chapter, we spoke about the need to know as much about your audience as possible. Now, within a myriad of constraints, it is time to create an environment that will prepare your audience for your presentation and, hopefully, encourage them to feel more receptive to your message.

Before you stand in front of an audience, familiarize yourself with the room you will be presenting in. At Sliding.ca we try to begin that familiarization process much farther afield than the room itself.

Your speaking venue doesn't only include the room you will be in, it can extend to the placement of the room within the building you are in, or where the building is in the city and whether it's easy for your audience to get to. There are a host of factors that are going to influence the mood and receptivity of your audience long before you begin your presentation: traffic, parking, weather, the distance people have to walk to get to you or the level of difficulty in finding the room, have they eaten or had coffee, etcetera. A little research can go a long way towards cluing you in to the head-space of your audience and provide you with the opportunity to alleviate any potential problems.

Look up the venue; if it looks like it would be a difficult place to get to, or there doesn't appear to be convenient parking, then it's a pretty good bet that your audience will arrive at the venue frustrated and less receptive to your message.

Whether a member of the audience or a presenter, we have all experienced the frustration of not being able to find the room we're looking for. At Sliding.ca we alleviate this problem by creating signs with arrows on them. Each of our signs have Sliding.ca printed right-side-up on the top of the sign and upside-down on the bottom of the sign so that they can be pointed in whichever direction we require. Just like laying a trail of bread crumbs we then scotch tape the signs to the walls showing people how to get to the venue — make sure you use tape that won't mar hotel walls because they hate it when you do that. As well as short-circuiting any potential frustration on the part of the audience the signs also serve as a sort of gentle embrace to audience members as they approach the venue, and, before the show even begins, show that you are thinking about their welfare.

Once you get into the room, try to get as familiar with it as possible. Do a complete walk around and figure out whether there are any line-of-sight issues or places where the sound may be a problem. For example, we conducted one seminar in particular in which Gerardo presented while I sat at the back of the room. I had to keep motioning to him to speak louder because, a short while after he began, air started rushing out of a vent over the heads of the back row of the audience making just enough noise to muffle everything he was saying. Needless to say, we now do our best to make sure no one sits under overhead fans or vents.

Always consider how you are going to use your stage. Make sure there's room to move and that there are no encumbrances to the flow of your movement or your gestures. Check to see whether the lectern is optimally placed for your purposes. If you plan to move into the audience at any time during your presentation make sure you have easy access from the stage to the floor and back again.

What's the temperature of the room? If it's too hot or too cold you might want to reset the thermostat or incorporate a break into your presentation to allow your audience to catch a breath of fresh air or to warm up a bit. Keep in mind, a room full of people can warm up quite quickly.

What's the seating like? Check out the seats in the audience. If the seats are uncomfortable you might consider introducing a well-timed exercise to get people moving around a little bit in order to get their circulation going. Conversely, if your presentation is a long one and the seating is too comfortable, like a room full of overstuffed sofas, you might want to get your audience up and moving so that they don't lose focus.

We believe in playing music as our audience enters the room. It really helps to set the mood[xiii] and, properly timed, serves as the perfect countdown to showtime. We also play music after our presentations. Just as it helps to set a mood before the show music can also be very effective in reinforcing and supporting the message shared by keeping the audience upbeat, or contemplative, or soothed, as the situation needs.

Remember, the stage is your workplace; you have every right, within reason, to arrange it to your benefit and to the benefit of your audience and the message you hope to share with them.

4.2 Visual vs. Auditory

The Battle of The Senses

Considering the fact that most lean toward the visual modality and some people lean toward the auditory modality, the one thing you can be sure of is that you risk having your message missed by a portion of your audience if you ignore either one of the visual - auditory modalities. Conversely, by fully covering both the visual and the auditory aspects of our presentation, we can increase the chances of reaching everyone in the audience.

> **Note**: Focusing on visual and auditory does not mean that you would exclude the other three senses. In general, the more of the audience's senses you can stimulate and appeal to, the better.

4.2.1 Visual

Seeing is Believing

The visual aspects of your presentation include everything your audience sees from the moment they enter the venue to the moment they leave. In an ideal situation, all they see will support and serve to promote and encourage them to fully and wholeheartedly embrace your message.

Let's consider which visual aspects of your venue you may have control over:

The room: Some presenters own or rent the venue they present in which allows them the luxury of creating the perfect environment for sharing their message. In most circumstances, though, the layout and décor of the room cannot be changed. That said, there are some things you might be able to control. You can usually control seating layout in order to best advantage sightlines or to influence your audience interaction. If the venue looks barren you may be able to bring along some portable banners to brighten up the room or hide distractions. As guests enter the venue a "welcome to our home" table can go a long way towards making people comfortable and embraced. Familiarize yourself with the lighting in the room, where the light switches are, and which switches work which lights. Light has a huge effect on mood[xiv] and, used creatively, can really help to prepare the audience for your presentation. Having a greeter at the door, or being a greeter yourself, also makes a big welcoming impression on guests; nothing beats being met with a big broad smile when walking into a new environment.

The stage: As a presenter, you may be allowed leeway when it comes to setting up your stage; if you are, take advantage of the opportunity. Make sure the stage has nothing on it that will distract from your message. Make sure everyone can see everything you want them to see and that, most importantly, they can see you.

The projection screen: Before you begin your presentation be sure to check the screen to ensure it is in focus and can be easily seen and read from any seat in the house. Depending on the lighting in the room you may want to adjust the brightness of the room to achieve maximum visibility. Nothing takes audience members out of the groove faster than having to squint or strain to see what's on the screen.

The presenter: The most important visual aspect of every presentation is you, the presenter. You are the show! Everything else involved in the presentation is there to support you. You are the message. Our decision-making process is, at its core, dominated by our emotions and nothing is more impactful than a meaningful interaction or connection with another human being. When presenting, you should do everything in your power to make that interaction as supportive of your goal as possible.

Dress to suit your audience and your topic. If you're presenting to a traditional business audience, jeans and a t-shirt might not be the best choice of dress. Likewise, if you're presenting on a holiday cruise ship to a group of swimsuit clad tourists a three-piece vested suit may not be your most fitting option.

The idea is, without pretending to be someone you're not, make your audience as receptive to you as possible.

Images are much easier to remember than words (Medina). Your job is to make that visual experience as stress free, pleasurable, and memorable as possible.

4.2.2 Auditory

"Friends, Romans, Countrymen, Lend Me Your Ears"
— William Shakespeare

The auditory aspects of your presentation include everything your audience hears from the moment they enter the venue to the moment they leave. In an ideal situation, everything they hear will support and serve to promote and encourage them to fully and wholeheartedly embrace your message.

Let's consider which auditory aspects of your venue you may have control over:

The room: Check out the entire room to get a sense of the acoustics you will be dealing with. Are there spots in the room where your audience might not hear as well as other audience members or where there may be other stimuli competing for your attention (noise from a kitchen, the street, an air conditioner, office equipment, etcetera). In situations like this you might be able to rearrange the seating or, at the very least, modulate your volume accordingly.

The stage: Check out your stage to see what the audio situation is. Will you be tethered to a stationary microphone or will you be wearing a body microphone enabling you the freedom to move around the room.

If you are forced to stay in one place and you are doing a slide show try to position yourself stage right of the projection screen (to the audience's left). We do this because, in western culture, we read from left to right. This means that, with every new thought, the audience will start with you and then move their gaze to the accompanying slide.

The audio equipment: If at all possible, try to avoid using a hand-held microphone to deliver your presentations. By using one, you will effectively be shutting down about half of your gestures. That is a huge amount of information you are denying your audience access to.

If possible, use a wireless headset microphone or body microphone (lavalier mic) so that you also have the freedom to move about the room without worrying about whether people can hear you or not.

The presenter: Just like with the visual, the most important auditory aspect of every presentation is you, because you are the show. As humans, we are genetically programmed to listen to and process the sound of the human voice.

In prehistoric times we would listen to a person speak while our primal brain was subconsciously assessing their volume, tone, intonation, rhythm, and pace in order to decide whether the person was friend or foe or a possible threat. While listening to a 21st Century presentation we might not be as concerned about whether the presenter is a friend or a foe, however, those subtle calculations are still being made. How the speaker's words affect the listener makes a huge difference when it comes to whether they will be receptive to the presenter's message. As best you can, and without belying who you are, try to get on the same wavelength as your audience and speak to them in a language, volume, tone, intonation, rhythm, and pace they will find familiar, comforting, and inspiring.

Even though your audience may be processing most of your information visually, the auditory portion is still critically important to the success of your presentation. Once again, your job is to make that information gathering experience as stress free as possible.

4.3 The Show

"A Little Bit of Stage Fright, Then I'm Ready"
— Faith Hill

Everything that happens on and off stage should further support your message. For audience members, the show begins the moment they enter the room and doesn't end until after they have left.

As a presenter, it is your responsibility to make that experience stimulating, pleasurable, and memorable.

4.3.1. Your Intro

The Long and Short of it

The success or failure of a presentation is often determined in the first few seconds of the show. If you begin tepidly, you risk losing your audience before you even get to your main message. This is why it is so important to quickly develop a rapport with your audience and establish yourself as somebody worth listening to.

The method you will use to begin your presentation will differ depending on whether you are doing a workshop/seminar or a traditional speech. What they have in common is the power of the pause.

The Power of the Pause

One of the main things an audience looks for in a speaker is confidence. The audience wants to know that they are in good hands and that what they are about to see won't make them feel uncomfortable or disappoint them.

In order to inspire confidence in your audience, this is what we suggest you do. When you first take your place on the stage, do nothing. Just stand there... quietly... pausing... for what may seem like an uncomfortable length of time... and gaze around the room making eye contact. Doing this accomplishes a number of things:

1. It gives the audience a few seconds to "get to know you." You are new to the audience, new to the stage, and new to the proceedings. The audience needs a second or two to size you up, look you over, and become accustomed to your presence (it's one of those reptilian brain, fight or flight things).

2. By standing still and doing nothing it draws the audience's attention to you so that you can begin with your audience focused on your first, all-important words.

3. Standing, quietly and confidently, without uttering a word, confers authority upon you, which calms the audience, and lets them know they are in good hands.

It must be noted that pauses are not only effective at the beginning of your delivery but, when used judiciously, can add power and poignancy to your speech or presentation.

When you speak with your audience (notice we said "speak *with* your audience" not "speak *to* your audience"), don't be afraid of lulls in the conversation. The pause is a very effective tool; learn to use it to your benefit. A pause can be an effective way to accent a point and give the audience time to think about what you have said and fully absorb your words. A pause can also be used to give you time to gather your thoughts, or change the rhythm of the conversation, or punctuate the end of a section of your talk. Once you get comfortable using pauses to your benefit, you will be able to speak to any audience, anytime, anywhere, without ever being afraid of being caught flat footed or lost for words.

Opening for a Workshop or Seminar

If you are conducting a workshop or a seminar, we suggest using the simple mnemonic (PARSE) to remind you of five simple steps that will make this process a little easier for you:

Pause (as described in The Power of the Pause).

Ask a question or take a poll. This step serves to engage the audience and gives you a chance to assess the audience's receptivity to your message and their level of knowledge regarding your topic.

When you ask a question, phrase it in a way that elicits an individual response and includes a physical action like a show of hands. For example, instead of simply asking "how *many* of you use a handheld mic?" raise your hand and ask "*by a show of hands,* do you use a handheld mic?" By doing this way, you will encourage each audience member to answer for themselves rather than counting hands and answering as a member of the herd. Additionally, by raising your hand and getting the audience to mirror your actions, you will increase your connection with them and enhance your position as team leader.

Recognize your audience. It is important that you let your audience know how much you appreciate their presence. By acknowledging them it also lets the audience know that you won't waste their time and that you will do all you can to provide them with a positive, valuable experience.

Share your personal story. By telling your own story you let the audience know that you are just like them. The only difference between you and them is that you possess a particular skill set or body of knowledge about the day's topic that you have gained over an extended period of time.

Explain what is about to happen. Let your audience know what's on the agenda, what housekeeping items they should be aware of, what they are going to learn, and how it's going to benefit them. During this step of the introduction, you will make your promise to the audience. It is imperative that your promise be reasonable, realistic and achievable. By delivering on that promise, you will send your audience home happy and satisfied, and deepen the bond you have created with them. It will also increase the chances that they will attend one of your other seminars or workshops and recommend you to others.

Opening for a Traditional Speech

When delivering a traditional speech, the first few seconds are even more critical. The audience must be engaged, stimulated, and enticed into wanting to hear more.

We believe every speech should begin with a clear, firm, unambiguous, statement. We refer to this as a "Launch-Pad Phrase." We call it a Launch-Pad Phrase because of the image it evokes of a countdown to an explosion of energy, followed by a rocket lifting to the heavens. For example, a controversial statement, a powerful rhetorical question, or an attention-grabbing statistic.

Here's how it works:

1. Pause… until it begins to feel awkward. This will draw the audience's attention to you and focussed on your opening words.

2. While you pause, focus on your Launch-Pad Phrase. This will help you to turn your nervous energy into positive energy.

3. When you are ready to speak… launch! Clearly, firmly, and unambiguously, state your Launch-Pad Phrase.

By using the Launch-Pad Phrase, you will grab your audience's attention, overcome your nervousness, and begin your speech with an energy that will set the tone for the rest of your speech.

> **Note:** Here's something to try just before you walk on stage to deliver your presentation. Stand up straight, take a few long deep breaths, raise the tip of your head to the sky, give your shoulders

and arms a shake, say to yourself: "That was fun, I really enjoyed that," and then walk on stage. Standing tall (some people call it a power stance) serves to give you the look and feel of confidence. Lifting your head to the sky will also help to increase your sense of self-confidence. Giving your shoulders and arms a shake will help to loosen you up before taking the stage. And, whispering: "That was fun, I really enjoyed that" to yourself serves to emotionally preordain good tidings for your performance and also serves to put a smile on your face before you greet your audience.

4.3.2 Stage Craft

Own the Stage

Staging includes everything you do on stage that influences what the audience sees, hears, and feels.

Seeing

Statistically, your audience is going to be, roughly, 75% visually dominant so what they see before them is going to be very important. Seeing includes everything your audience sees you do, from eye contact, to how you move, to your gestures. Let's take a look at all three.

Eye Contact

As you speak with your audience try to maintain eye contact with them. Eye contact creates a bond[xv]. It is the first step in building a connection with those you are speaking with and helping them to accept and embrace your message.

To make it easier to establish and maintain eye contact here's a simple two-step process to consider as you interact with your audience:

1. As you first walk onto the stage, split your audience into three sections (left, centre, and right), or six sections if it is a large room (left front, left back, centre front, centre back, right front, and right back).

2. As you present, make a point of making eye contact with and speaking to individual people in each of the above sections.

Each time you focus on one person in a section it, not only, lets that person and the people in their section know they are being spoken to, it lets the rest of the audience see and know that you're interacting on a personal level. Using this method will also help you to avoid the habit of scanning the audience without actually looking anyone in the eye.

This is a very effective technique even when speaking from behind a lectern.

Movement

How you move on stage is very important. Used properly, movement will imbue your presentation with a sense of energy and poise. However, too much movement can make you look indecisive and hurried, something often referred to as the: "Caged tiger syndrome".

Now that you have divided the audience into three sections, think of your stage as also being divided into three sections. These areas are stage-right, centre-stage, stage-left. These three distinct sections will serve a very important purpose as you share your story with your audience and take them with you on your journey.

As you move through your presentation you will begin at centre-stage (as long as you're not blocking the projection), move to stage-right, move back to centre-stage, move to stage-left, and then move back to centre-stage to conclude your talk.

Here are the five steps involved in effective movement:

1. Begin at centre-stage. This is where you present your introduction and prepare to take the audience on the journey.

2. Next step, move stage-right (stage-right is to your right as you face the audience). From stage-right you will present point number one of your talk. Point number one can represent the past, the problem, a location, a point of view, or whatever best represents the first point you want to make.

3. To present point number two you will move to centre-stage. Point number two can represent the present, the solution to the problem, a new location, a differing point of view, or whatever best represents the second point you want to make.

4. To present point number three you will move stage-left. Point number three can represent the future, the actions

necessary to solve the problem, a final location, a final point of view, or whatever best represents the third point you want to make.

5. To close your presentation, sum up all you've talked about, and make your final entreaty to the audience, return to centre-stage.

By going through these five distinct steps your audience benefits in a number of ways: 1. They get to go on a metaphorical journey with you that they not only hear but see. 2. They have an easier time delineating and remembering the three different points you have presented during your talk. 3. They get to experience a presentation that has variety rather than just a talking head. 4. They get to interact and connect with you on a more personal level because you have physically moved closer to them on stage at different points in your talk.

> **Note**: The reason we start our journey by moving from stage-right to centre-stage and then to stage-left is: In western culture, we read from left to right; this predisposes an audience to think in terms of moving forward from left to right, the past being on their left and the future being on their right. This progression works the same for each of the points in your talk with one point following the other, literally, and in the audience's mind.
>
> Keep in mind that the audience's point of view is the reverse of the presenter, and that this rule should be reversed in cultures that read from right to left.

Gestures

As you stand before your audience don't be afraid to use broad gestures. Your gestures never look as large to the audience as they feel to you. Larger gestures bring life to a talk and help to convey a great deal of information. A trap that speakers often fall into is the "T-Rex syndrome." This is where the speaker's elbows seem glued to their body and the resultant effect is that of a dinosaur flailing about with short, stubby little hands and arms. T-Rex hands look odd and very stilted so don't be afraid to be expansive in your gestures.

Hearing

Every time you speak it is crucial that your words be heard and listened to. If the audience can't hear you, they will stop listening and, if they aren't listening, they definitely won't be accepting and embracing of your message. To overcome this problem, you must learn to improve your vocal variety and voice projection.

Vocal Variety. Vocal variety helps to keep a talk interesting and lively. The ups and downs of the story can be enhanced or highlighted with changes in tone, pitch, or pace. Imagine the difference between listening to a story being told in a boring monotone voice compared to a story being told with intensity and gusto. It is obvious which story would most likely capture your attention. By bringing enthusiasm to your speaking style, you will immeasurably increase your audience's attention level and their enjoyment of your speech.

Voice Projection. Many people think that voice projection and volume are the same thing, but they are not. Volume is about decibel level, while voice projection is about the intention, on the part of the speaker, to be heard and clearly understand. Speakers often make this mistake and think, to be heard by their audience, all they have to do is speak louder. Unfortunately, there is a limit to how loud a person's voice can get before it becomes annoying.

At Sliding.ca we leave volume improvement to the many vocal coaches out there who are much better equipped to deal with that issue than we are. However, when it comes to improving vocal projection, there's a simple technique that works wonders towards overcoming the problem of not being heard. Here is what to do:

Before speaking tell yourself that there are one or two people in the back row of the audience that absolutely, positively, and unconditionally, must hear and understand your message. Adopting this attitude will change how you speak. It will encourage you to speak louder, more clearly, with more gestures, more eye contact, and to the entire room rather than just the first few rows.

Feeling

Presenting is about connecting. To do this, use your eyes, your voice, and also your gestures. Just as we suggested using your gestures to enhance your story you can also use them to increase your connection with your audience.

Reach out and into your audience. When people speak in public, they often picture an invisible demarcation line between themselves and the audience. In order to fully connect with your audience, this imaginary demarcation line has to be breached. You do this by reaching across it.

As you make points during your speech, include questions in your talk and, physically, reach out to the audience for answers. By doing this you will erase that pesky demarcation line and get the energy flowing back and forth between you and your audience. When that happens, you've got real connection.

As you move from place to place on the stage, it is important to make your movements seem smooth and as natural as possible. A strategy that will help you to accomplish this, is what we call "The Fishing Method." Here is how it works:

As you move from one section of the stage to another, address the first sentence of the next part of your speech to an individual audience member. As you do this, reach out and move towards that person as if you are sharing information with them because it is vital that they hear and absorb what is being said. Even though you are addressing one particular individual, that person will serve as a proxy for everyone else in the audience and make it clear that you are interested in interacting and connecting with each and every member of the audience.

Remember, we are heavily influenced by our emotions. If you do not reach out and inspire your audience, they will be much less likely to accept and embrace your message.

> **Note**: As you move from one section of the stage to another (centre, right, left) don't forget to continue to make eye contact with each of the three sections of your audience. Just because you are stage-right doesn't mean you can forget about interacting with the people sitting far to your left. It is vitally important that EVERYONE in your audience feel important and included in your talk.

4.3.3 Be Magical

*Capture the Imagination...
Hearts and Minds Will Follow*

One of the greatest challenges presenters face is cutting through the overwhelming amount of information that constantly bombards us.

At Sliding.ca, one of the strategies we use to overcome this ever-present problem is to include in our presentations what we call magical beats.

What is a magical beat? A magical beat is a moment in a presentation when something a little out of the ordinary happens. It is that point in time that engages the audience in a different way and serves to stand out from the rest of the presentation.

Magical beats can take the form of a game, an exercise, or it can be something silly yet memorable that breaks the routine of what has come before that point in the presentation.

The point of the magical beat is to interrupt the normal rhythm of the event in a way that the audience will find unforgettable. A perfect magical beat will place the presenter's main message front and centre before the audience so that it stands out from the rest of the presentation like a neon sign shining brightly in the listener's memory.

In order to create an effective magical beat, you should try to involve as many of the audience's senses as possible. Each time you involve a different one of the listener's senses you create a new opportunity to anchor and impress your message upon that individual. Imagine getting your audience to remember your message not only through their sense of sight and hearing but also through touch, taste, and smell.

Used properly, a magical beat will also serve to support and further your metaphor. Your goal in a presentation is to have everything you do and say reinforce everything else you do and say in the presentation. If you can get everything working together (your main message, your metaphor, your syntax, your magical beat) you will have created an experience that the audience will remember forever.

4.3.4 Speaking with Emotion

> *"There can be no Transforming of Darkness into Light nor Apathy into Movement without Emotion"*
> — Carl Jung

Nothing connects a presenter with their audience more than the sharing of honest emotion.[xvi] Properly placed, it can exponentially increase the impact a speaker has on his/her audience. Unfortunately, standing in front of a group of people is already scary, and sharing your emotions with them can make it even scarier. The fear is that, once you allow yourself to get emotional, you might not be able to get back on track.

At Sliding.ca, a simple trick we use to overcome this problem is to create and use a safe word. Here's how it works. Choose a safe word that you wouldn't normally use in your speech writing or everyday conversation (one of our clients uses the word broccoli) and combine it with a strategy that psychologists suggest people adopt in order to control bouts of anger[xvii]. When people find themselves getting angry and losing control, you will often hear the suggestion that they count from one to ten and take a breath. The purpose of counting from one to ten is to interrupt the person's behaviour and give them an opportunity to reset their emotional state.

By using your safe word, you are, essentially, doing the same thing. When delivering a speech, you don't have time to stop and count from one to ten, but you do have time to silently say your safe word to yourself, interrupt your emotion, take a breath, reset your emotional state, and continue your presentation.

Now that you've chosen a safe word and you understand how the process works, it is time to practice and internalize its use. To practice using your safe word create a situation for yourself (like watching a movie or listening to music) that moves you emotionally. Then, as you feel the emotion begin to affect you, use your safe word to interrupt the emotion, take a breath and do it again. With practice, you will develop your ability to speak with honest, heartfelt emotion, confident in the knowledge that your safe word is always with you if you need it.

Choose your safe word and master its use; you will be pleasantly surprised.

4.3.5 The Close

Leave Them Wanting to Know More

The close of your presentation is of utmost importance. This is the last moment you will have to speak with your audience, and connect with them, before they return to their own lives.

Moving back to centre-stage is the moment when you:

1. Reiterate the main message you came to share.

2. Restate the points in support of that main message

3. Deliver the all-important call to action.

Keep in mind, during a closing statement your goal isn't to *persuade* the audience to act, your goal is to *inspire* the audience to act.

Just as you did throughout the entire process of preparing your presentation, and just as you did as you delivered the body of your presentation, you should constantly be in a "what's in it for them?" mindset.

Your language, your gestures, your emotionality, should take your audience to a higher level. To use an analogy, think of your presentation as if it were a church service and your closing statement is the benediction. This is the moment when you do everything in your power to send your listeners home feeling better about themselves, their potential, and their future. And, wrapped in that benediction, and all the positivity that surrounds it, will be your call to action, bathed in goodness, light, and unlimited possibilities.

You have taken the audience on a journey. You have guided them from your opening statement, to a first, second, and third point, and finally to this better place. Enlightened, energized, and empowered, they are now ready to move forward, share, and act upon what they have learned.

You're done. Thank your audience and pause. Be sure you don't leave the stage too quickly. The slow, calm, demeanour you exhibited at the beginning of your presentation conveyed confidence and authority to your audience. Now, by calmly taking a moment to absorb the audience's reaction to your presentation, regardless of how they responded, and then slowly leaving the stage you will reinforce that aura of confidence and authority and add gravitas to everything the audience has seen, heard, and felt.

Remember, from the moment a person walks into the venue to the moment they walk out they are participating in a show created and orchestrated to inform, entertain, and inspire them. As a presenter it is your job to make that experience as informative, entertaining, and inspiring as possible. Do that with passion and honesty and it's a win, win!

4.4 The 3G Method

Any Audience, Anytime, Anywhere

At Sliding.ca, some of the people we help don't often speak in public or, in some cases, virtually never speak in public. To accommodate the occasional speaker, we have created a stand-alone program that we call: "The 3G-Method."

The 3G-Method consists of three components: The Gift, The Gifter, and The Giftee. It is designed to help novice speakers overcome their fear and nervousness and make it easier for them to stand before a group and share a message. We do this by focussing, in the first and third components (The Gift and The Giftee) on the speaker's attitude and relationship with their audience. We then consolidate these strategies with the second component (The Gifter) which consists of a selection of tips that we've covered in previous chapters.

Although the 3G-Method is designed to help novice speakers, the strategies it espouses can be of benefit to speakers of all skill levels.

Here's how it works:

The **Gift**: A speaker or presenter's gift is the **main message** they hope to share with their audience. And, like every gift, it should be estimable, beneficial, and given from the heart.

There is nothing more powerful than the honest belief that your gift could transform the life of someone in your audience.

Creating and honing an estimable and beneficial message that is also clear, concise, and compelling, can be an arduous process. However, once the hard work is completed, that main message will serve to keep the speaker on track, provide a standard to measure all other content against, and serve as a lodestar to guide the speaker to that "better place" she or he is taking the audience to.

The attitude the speaker must now adopt is the firm, unshakeable belief in the value of the gift they are about to share with their audience. It is this sincere belief in the value of the gift (the main message) that allows the speaker to shift their focus away from themselves and onto the sharing of the information they believe will benefit the members of their audience.

Conversely, if the speaker cannot sincerely believe in the main message they are about to share, they will have to go back and hone it, change it, improve it, or throw it out and start over. A gift worthy of an audience's time and attention is absolutely necessary if a speaker ever hopes to have their message listened to, remembered, and embraced.

DELIVERY

The **Gifter**: In this section, we use the word gifter as a substitute for the word speaker because it helps to remind the presenter that they are delivering a gift to their audience. Although we've already discussed some of the information presented here it doesn't hurt to go through it again in the context of the 3G-Method.

As we've discussed previously, the first of these simple strategies is to take the stage and, silently, divide the audience into three distinct sections (right – centre – left). By doing this you will accomplish a number of things:

1. By proactively dividing the audience into three sections, even though the gesture is performed silently, the speaker "does something to the audience" and, by doing so, confers upon themselves a measure of control they didn't have when they first walked on stage.

2. A segmented audience feels less daunting than a larger audience which, to a novice speaker, can seem very intimidating.

3. A segmented audience is easier to maintain eye contact with than a full audience. Speakers who view an audience as though it is one large group often end up scanning the group instead of making eye contact with individual audience members. Making eye contact with an individual lets them know that you are trying to connect with them and, by proxy, demonstrates to every other member of the audience that you are trying to connect with them as well.

The second of these simple strategies is to select a couple of people, sitting apart from each other, at the back of the room and internalize the belief that it is positively imperative that they hear and absolutely understand the main message. The internalization of this attitude will result in the presenter speaking louder, more emphatically, and with greater enunciation to the people at the back of the room and, collaterally, with every other member of the audience. This desire to make sure those people hear and absolutely understand the main message gives rise to two other significant benefits. By reaching out to those audience members at the back of the room, speakers will find that they end up gesturing more broadly and making eye contact with many more members of the audience.

Thirdly, when moving from one area of the stage to another make eye contact with a member of the audience and speak directly to them. This simple little strategy makes it seem as though it was the act of speaking to that audience member that provided the impetus for the move rather than it being a preplanned decision. Consequently, the speaker will look as though they are being reactive to, and interactive with, the audience.

The **Giftee**: Earlier, we spoke about the power of believing in the value of your gift. Now, it is time to firmly believe that there is, at least, one member of your audience whose life will be improved by hearing, remembering, and embracing the main message you are about to share. If you have any trouble at all mustering this belief in your main message you will have to go back and tweak it, improve it, or throw it out and start over. However, once you have a main message you can embrace, the belief you have in that message will provide you with a tool that can turn a good speech into a great speech.

Belief in your gift will turn what began as a daunting challenge into a rare opportunity to share something wonderful with a group of your peers. Get out there and actively search for the person, or persons, in your audience whose life you can improve.

By internalizing this simple attitude, you turn your presentation into an active, enthusiastic, embracing experience for your audience. You will find yourself making more eye contact, reaching out more, and truly connecting with your audience and feeling their energy.

The same way focusing on your gift helps you to calm your nerves and look outward, searching for that giftee in the audience will help you rise above your nervousness. You will find yourself putting aside your fears, enthusiastically reaching out to your audience, and endeavouring to share something of value that will take people to a better place. What a thrill!

If you are a novice speaker embrace the 3G Method. We believe it is, by far, the most effective technique for newcomers to overcome their fear of speaking in public. If you are a seasoned speaker, the 3G Method will, undoubtedly, serve to raise your skills to a higher level.

Either way, the 3G Method rocks.

The Online World

When we deliver to an audience from a stage, we strive to make every person in the audience feel as though we are speaking to them personally.

When we speak to people online, every person in the audience sees your face up close, making it feel as though you are speaking only to them.

What's missing is the flow of energy that occurs when people speak face to face, and the subtleties of body language and audience response available to us in a more intimate setting.

Here are several things we can do to compensate for this lack of human-to-human energy.

The Session

1. Before you begin your session:

  1.1 **Mentally prepare** for and review the material that you intend to share with your audience.

  1.2 **Have water** or a refreshment ready and close at hand so you don't feel the need to leave the stage.

  1.3 Be aware that chequered or thin striped clothing can make your camera do weird things (it's called the **Moiré Effect**).

  1.4 **Close all unnecessary software**, such as email or messaging apps.

2. **As you begin your session:**

    2.1. **Welcome all members**, thank them for attending, and establish a congenial atmosphere with safe chit-chat.

    2.2. **Introduce the participants** in order to break the ice and to create an atmosphere of familiarity and trust.

    2.3. **Take care of housekeeping** by explaining to participants how to mute and activate their microphones and cameras, and use the non-verbal interaction tools (polls, the raise-hand button, yes/no buttons, etcetera).

    2.4. Some participants may want to leave their **camera off**; consider that there may be a good reason for them to do that.

    2.5. **Don't speak for long periods** of time without something happening on the screen.

    2.6. Online, you are limited in how much you can physically show the audience, so it's important to **be clear, concise, and descriptive** when you speak.

3. **As your session progresses:**

    3.1. **Stick to the agenda**.

    3.2. Always try to maintain proper **netiquette**.

    3.3. **Stay engaged** with your audience and endeavour to make everyone feel included in the conversation.

3.4. Throughout your session, always **be a good host** and treat your audience as if they were guests you've invited into your home.

3.5. Every 10 to 15 minutes, **introduce an activity**, such as a Quiz, Q&A, Discussion, or Reflection. You can use tools like:

- AnswerGarden
- Forms
- Kahoot
- Mentimeter
- Nearpod
- Poll Everywhere
- Socrative

The Presenter

4. **As you present:**

   4.1. **Don't sit too close to the camera**; it could distort your facial features.

   4.2. **Don't sit too far from the camera**; it could hamper your connection with your audience.

   4.3. **Look into the camera.** If possible, select a layout in which the participant's faces are close to your camera, so when you look at them, your eye line will be closer to theirs.

4.4. **Don't keep shifting positions**; it can be distracting or make you look fidgety and bored.

4.5. **Be an active listener** by occasionally nodding or indicating in some way that you are engaged in the conversation.

4.6. **Avoid doing other things**, such as checking your email, browsing the internet, texting, etcetera.

4.7. Unless you have a compelling reason (such as low blood sugar), **don't eat on camera**.

4.8. Don't forget to **mute if you have to step away**.

5. **Verbally**

    5.1. **Speak clearly**.

    5.2. Try to **be conversational**.

    5.3. **Use descriptive language**.

    5.4. **Modulate your tone**; nothing puts people to sleep faster than a droning monotone.

    5.5. **Vary your pace and rhythm**.

    5.6. Don't be afraid to **add pauses**; they give your audience time to absorb what you are saying and can also be effective in adding gravitas to an idea or concept.

    5.7. **Be aware of your voice**. After speaking to a baby or a pet, don't make the mistake of continuing to speak to your online audience in that baby or pet voice.

6. Visually

6.1. Remember, just as in a live presentation, **you are the message**.

6.2. Always try to **be well-groomed**; it shows respect.

6.3. **Dress appropriately** for the audience you are speaking to.

6.4. **Maintain your enthusiasm**; the camera picks up everything.

6.5. **Use gestures** and make sure they are visible to the audience.

6.6. **Do not lean on your desk**; it can make you look distorted and bored.

Case Study: Use The 3G Method

When we got a call from Ana, the main challenge she faced was an extremely tight timeline. Ana had been asked to do a presentation for the members of the sales force she was a part of with less than a day's preparation. The tea company she worked for had a new product to unveil. Ana's job was to introduce the new product to the sales team, explain its features and benefits, and then inspire them to fully embrace the new item as a part of the product line they would sell to their customers. This was a perfect situation to utilize our 3G Method. We designed the 3G Method to help people who don't have a lot of time to prepare or don't have the opportunity to practice their public speaking regularly. For clients in these types of situations, the challenge faced is more about overcoming nervousness and finding a way to connect with the audience than it is about the content of the presentation. Ana was familiar with the product being unveiled so our goal was to help her to better understand the wants and needs of her audience, provide her with a format she could work within that would give her the confidence to be herself, and then equip her with some elements of stagecraft designed to make her look and feel more comfortable on stage and help her to increase her connection with her audience.

To accomplish this goal, we introduced Ana to The Gift, The Gifter, and The Giftee — the three main elements of the 3G Method.

The Gift would be Ana's prime message to her audience, that the company's new product would help the sales team to increase their sales figures and make their lives easier.

We then showed Ana, **The Gifter**, three elements of stagecraft (movement, eye contact, and volume) she could use to make it easier for her audience to remember her message. We showed Ana how to:

1. Move from point to point on the stage.

2. Improve eye contact with the audience by segmenting her audience into left, centre, and right.

3. Increase her volume and clarity of speech by choosing a member of the audience sitting farthest from the stage, and making sure that person could hear and understand every single word.

The Giftee. To intensify Ana's connection with her audience we asked her to internalize the belief that there would be at least, one member of her audience whose life would be improved by hearing, remembering, and embracing the main message she was about to share with them. Then, once that belief had been internalized, we asked her to actively, with her gestures, her eyes, and her words, search the audience for the person whose life she was about to improve.

When all was said and done, Ana's presentation was a hit with the members of her sales team, and her boss was more than complimentary to her.

The 3G Method works.

Points to Consider

- Every aspect of the environment is a part of the show.

- Audiences tend to be visually dominant.

- As a presenter, it is your responsibility to make your audience's experience stimulating, pleasurable, and memorable.

- Speak *with* your audience, not *to* your audience.

- Bond with your audience through eye contact.

- Be big on the stage.

- Don't be afraid to share an emotional moment with your audience.

- Embrace the 3G Method.

5. CONCLUSION

"Every New Beginning Comes from Some Other Beginning's End"

— Seneca

We have reached the culmination of our discourse; this is where we close and present our call to action.

Let's get started, or finished, depending on your point of view.

5.1 The 5Cs

The Speaker's Ascent

After observing and working with speakers, from novice to expert, we have noticed a progression of levels that all speakers appear to go through as they develop their skills and become better communicators.

The labels we have placed on these five levels provide speakers with landmarks they can aspire to as they progress. Conveniently, each level just happens to start with the letter c; which is why we call them the 5Cs. Here they are:

Control: When a novice speaker comes to us for help the first challenge they face is overcoming the basic fear that the great majority of the population feels when asked to stand before an audience and speak. We call this the Control stage in that their biggest fear is they will, literally, not be able to control their body. This lack of control can manifest itself in many different ways, from physically shaking with nervousness, to losing one's voice, to fainting on stage.

Often, speakers working at this basic level would not normally be called upon, or ever want, to stand before an audience and speak. However, through circumstances beyond their control, they have suddenly found themselves thrust into the spotlight in order to deliver a wedding speech, a eulogy at a funeral, their first business presentation, or some other type of once-in-a-lifetime speech.

Confidence: After learning to control the basic fear of standing before an audience, it is time for the speaker to learn about and improve their vocal variety, use of gestures, and stagecraft. By mastering these basic skills, the speaker will improve their confidence level and free themselves up to focus on the message they hope to share with their audience.

Confidence is a trait no public speaker can do without. The last thing an audience wants to do is fret over whether a speaker is going to make it through their speech or not. It is very uncomfortable to sit in an audience and feel like you are about to see someone face a crisis, no matter how small.

Conversation: Speeches and presentations are transactions. The speaker/presenter stands on stage and, tacitly or overtly, asks for an audience's attention. In return for that attention the speaker agrees to entertain, inform, or inspire (ideally, every presentation will contain a combination of all three of these motivators).

Most successful transactions are ones that move back and forth between the parties involved. At the Conversation level, even though no words may actually be spoken by members of the audience, a skilled communicator will make everyone in the audience feel as if they are a part of that transaction and that the speaker is being receptive and responsive to them.

When a speaker is performing at the Conversation level there's a feeling that the invisible line that separates the audience from the stage has been eliminated and the energy is flowing backwards and forwards between the speaker and the audience. Whether words are being spoken by one person or more than one person, a conversation is taking place.

Connection: Connection with the audience takes place when the speaker and his/her audience feel as though they are on the same wavelength and sharing a common energy. When a connection is achieved the bond between the audience and the speaker becomes exponentially stronger than it is at the Conversation level. Events where both speaker and audience feel connected hum with energy; they are a joy to be a part of.

Communion: Communion with an audience is the ultimate bond a speaker and their audience can hope to attain. It enters the realm of the spiritual and is something you would rarely find outside a church service or similar type of ritualized celebration. However, under the right circumstances, it can be attained. When the Communion level is reached everyone in attendance leaves the event affected, changed, and hopefully, improved. It is rare, exhilarating, life changing, and a level worthy of aspiration.

As you move up through these five levels, practice and internalize all you have learned and don't be afraid to try new things.

Ascending from tier to tier, you will realize you are not only improving your speaking and communication skills, you are increasing your capacity for relating to others and, in some small way, contributing to their happiness and their joy.

Lofty words, perhaps; but well worth the investment of time, energy, and imagination.

Case Study: Dream of Communion

On June 26, 2015, President Barack Obama delivered a eulogy at the funeral of Reverend Clementa Pinckney, one of nine victims murdered by a gunman at the Emanuel African Methodist Episcopal Church in Charleston, South Carolina. President Obama was fully connected with the congregation and well into his eulogy when, near the end of his talk, his connection turned to communion. During the final moments of President Obama's speech, he paused, said nothing for about ten seconds, and then began quietly singing the Christian hymn Amazing Grace. The response from the congregation was immediate. They stood and sang along with President Obama, and it was electric. Even watching the event on television, you could feel the emotion. Every person in that church, and the millions of people watching from around the world, understood and felt what President Obama was feeling. There was communion among them. Check out the video, it was an exceptional moment.

Communion rarely happens but when it does, it is a deeply moving and memorable experience... a goal worth striving for.

5.2 Our Call to Action

"All the World's a Stage"
—William Shakespeare

We wrote this book so that we could share a panoply of tools, tips, and teachings that we believe will help you to become a better public speaker or presenter.

We also believe that many of the topics we've talked about apply to much more than presenting and can be applied to your life in ways that go far beyond simply communicating data or ideas.

We entreat you: explore these ideas, parse them, dissect them, reform the concepts we've shared, and come up with new ideas and new concepts.

We all have gifts to share… get gifting!

Thank you for reading our book. We hope you enjoyed the journey and we sincerely hope you will find value in our gift. Please don't just read our book just once; use it as a reference and revisit it again and again as you progress on your own personal journey towards becoming a better, more skilled, and more embraced public speaker and presenter.

Cheers,

Testimonials

Patrick and Gerardo taught me how to confidently and naturally converse with a group of individuals rather than stiffly present to an audience. What a difference... for me and the listeners! I would recommend Sliding.ca to anyone looking to create and deliver an impactful presentation.

- Larry Bates, financial advisor and author

The assistance Sliding.ca provided us in our procurement of funds for our educational program has been fundamental, to say the least. As we approached global financial institutions, such as JPMorgan, the development of a strong and clear message, accompanied by supporting points and an effective strategy was vital. This would have been very difficult for us without the help of the extraordinary team at Sliding.ca

- María Clara Gaviria, business owner and entrepreneur

The Perfect Presentations seminar proved to be incredibly helpful. The learning provided us with the necessary skills to transmit our ideas to a wide array of audiences, in an effective and organized fashion. I highly recommend this seminar to those organizations that seek to become more strategic in their communication with their internal and external customers.

- Danny Antezana, Senior Director, Global Supply Chain

I have always been successful but never to the extent that I desired. I hired Gerardo and Patrick to coach me in setting up my next corporate presentation. WOW was I impressed! Sliding.ca offers full end-to-end services to prepare a communication package that will remain memorable and the springboard for unexpected professional opportunities.

I could go on and on... but let me end with that I was never so well prepared and excited to go outside of my comfort zone... with unprecedented benefits.

- Danièle Thibodeau, PhD, PMP, DTM.

Sliding.ca helped me to organize my ideas. The results are simply inspiring. Today I can create an impact with slides that previously I was unaware I had the capability of.

- Roman Smolak, DTM, IT sector sales executive

I received extraordinary coaching from the Sliding.ca team in preparation for a major presentation I recently delivered at a conference in Cleveland. In fact, they changed my whole method for preparing and presenting to a large public audience. They coached me to change my tried and true "safe" style of preparation to the SLIDING method that resulted in a dynamic presentation — exciting and light-years ahead of traditional methods. I felt like I had joined the 21st Century of presenters. The response from my audience was instant and sustained. They loved it, and they really got my message. I'll never go back!

- Karen Lynn, language coach and college professor

About Us

Our guiding principle...
To help others to raise their potential through improved communication skills.

Sliding.ca is the brainchild of friends who share a passion for public speaking. In 2010, two years after meeting through our local Toastmasters club, we were sitting down together at our favourite coffee shop when the conversation turned to goals and dreams.

As we began expressing surprisingly similar visions for our future, we decided to work together to help each other realize those dreams. We began formulating a game plan (literally on a napkin) for what would become Sliding.ca.

By combining life experience with our various backgrounds in teaching and training we recognized what we had before us was the kernel of a unique approach to an age-old question:

> What does it take to create a presentation the audience will remember long after the show is over?

Image Credits

(Uncredited images by Sliding.ca)

Introduction

- Packaged food aisles in an Oregonian hypermarket — By Original: lyzadangerDerivative work: Diliff - https://www.flickr.com/photos/lyza/49545547, CC BY-SA 2.0, https://commons.wikimedia.org/w/index.php?curid=1405631

Content

- Hot Air Balloon by Cleverpix from pixabay.com

- Kitchen by Gerardo Suarez del Real

- XX. The Shinkansen N700A Series Set G13 high speed train travelling at approximately 300 km/h through Himeji Station, by Dllu - Own work, CC BY-SA 4.0, https://commons.wikimedia.org/w/index.php?curid=62705630

Delivery

- Gerardo presenting for the Professional Engineers of Ontario (PEO) at the University of Toronto by Patrick Williams

Conclusion

- President Barack Obama delivers the eulogy at the funeral of Reverend Clementa Pinckney at the College of Charleston in Charleston, S.C., June 26, 2015. (Official White House Photo by Lawrence Jackson)

References

Duarte, Nancy. *Resonate*. Hoboken: John Wiley / Sons, Inc., 2010.

—. *slide:ology*. Sebastopol: O'Reily Media, Inc., 2008.

Few, Stephen. *Show Me the Numbers*. Burlingame: Analytics Press, 2012.

Marks, Terry, Mine, and Sutton, Tina. *Color Harmony Compendium : A Complete Color Reference for Designers of All Types, 25th Anniversary Edition*. Osceola, WI, USA: Rockport, 2009.

Medina, John. *Brain Rules*. Seattle: Pear Press, 2008.

Reynolds, Garr. *Presentation Zen Design, Second Edition*. New Riders, 2014.

Tufte, Edward R. *The Visual Display of Quantitative Information 2nd. Ed.* Cheshire: Graphic Press, 2001.

Endnotes

[i] Balazs, Katharina. *What Leaders can Learn from both Clinton and Trump*. Fountainebleau: INSEAD, 2016. *ProQuest*. Web. 1 Feb. 2018.

[ii] Miller, Matt. *Is Persuasion Dead?* The New York Times, http://www.nytimes.com/2005/06/04/opinion/is-persuasion-dead.html. 4 June 2005

[iii] GAL, DAVID, and DEREK D. RUCKER. "Answering the Unasked Question: Response Substitution in Consumer Surveys." *Journal of Marketing Research*, vol. 48, no. 1, 2011, pp. 185–195. *JSTOR*, JSTOR, www.jstor.org/stable/25764573.

[iv] BECHARA, A., DAMASIO, H. and DAMASIO, A. R. (2003), Role of the Amygdala in Decision-Making. Annals of the New York Academy of Sciences, 985: 356–369. doi:10.1111/j.1749-6632.2003.tb07094.x

[v] https://en.oxforddictionaries.com/word-of-the-year/word-of-the-year-2016

[vi] Von Ahn, Luis, et al. "ReCAPTCHA: Human-Based Character Recognition via Web Security Measures." *Science*, vol. 321, no. 5895, 2008, pp. 1465–1468. *JSTOR*, JSTOR, www.jstor.org/stable/20144795.

[vii] Doran, George T. "There's a S.M.A.R.T. way to write management's goals and objectives." *Management Review* November, 1981

[viii] Lamm, Jean Decety and Claus. "Human Empathy Through the Lens of Social Neuroscience." *The Scientific World JOURNAL* 6 (2006): 1146-1163.g

[ix] Gallo, Carmine. *https://www.inc.com/carmine-gallo/jeff-bezos-bans-powerpoint-in-meetings-his-replacement-is-brilliant.html*. 25 April 2018. 3 May 2018.

[x] McLuhan, Marshall. "Understanding Media: The Extensions of Man." *The Medium is the Message*. 1964. http://web.mit.edu/allanmc/www/mcluhan.mediummessage.pdf.

[xi] Brock, David C. "The improbable origins of Powerpoint." *IEEE Spectrum* Vol.54(11) (2017): 42-49.

[xii] Arditi, Aries and Jianna Cho. "Serifs and font legibility." *Vision Research* 45.23 (2005): 2926-2933.

xiii Krahé, Barbara, and Steffen Bieneck. "The Effect of Music-Induced Mood on Aggressive Affect, Cognition, and Behavior1." *Journal of Applied Social Psychology* 42.2 (2012): 271-90. Web.

xiv Küller R., Ballal S., Laike T., Mikellides B., Tonello G. "The impact of light and colour on psychological mood: a cross-cultural study of indoor work environments." *PubMed.gov* (2006). https://www.ncbi.nlm.nih.gov/pubmed/17050390

xv Senju, and Johnson. "The Eye Contact Effect: Mechanisms and Development." Trends in Cognitive Sciences 13.3 (2009): 127-34. Web.

xvi Jean Decety and Claus Lamm, "Human Empathy Through the Lens of Social Neuroscience," TheScientificWorldJOURNAL, vol. 6, pp. 1146-1163, 2006. https://doi.org/10.1100/tsw.2006.221.

xvii Sorgen, Carol. *Anger Management: Counting to 10 and Beyond.* 6 4 2006. 4 5 2018. https://www.webmd.com/sex-relationships/features/anger-management-counting-to-ten#1

www.ingramcontent.com/pod-product-compliance
Lightning Source LLC
Chambersburg PA
CBHW031921240526
45464CB00021B/620